Learie Constantine

Caribbean Lives

Learie Constantine

Peter Mason

MACMILLAN
CARIBBEAN

Signal

Macmillan Education
Between Towns Road, Oxford OX4 3PP
A division of Macmillan Publishers Limited
Companies and representatives throughout the world

www.macmillan-caribbean.com

ISBN: 978-1-4050-8173-3

First published in 2008

First published in the UK in 2008 by
Signal Books Limited
36 Minster Road
Oxford OX4 1LY
ISBN: 978-1-904955-42-9

Designed by Mike Brain Graphic Design Ltd
Typeset by EXPO Holdings
Cover design by Andy Esson at Baseline
Cover photograph by Topfoto

The author and publishers would like to thank the following for permission to
reproduce their photographs:
Corbis / Bettman Archive pp26, 60, 98, 193
Getty / Hulton Archive pp21, 34, 92, 104, 109, 135, 171
P.A Photos pp42, 56
Topfoto pp title page, 1, 23, 54, 76, 100, 128, 150, 153, 180, 184
Watford Observer p125

These materials may contain links for third party websites. We have no
control over, and are not responsible for, the contents of such third
party websites. Please use care when accessing them.

Printed and bound in Malaysia

2012 2011 2010 2009 2008
10 9 8 7 6 5 4 3 2 1

Dedication

To Amelia Scarlett

When the moment comes
And the gathering stands
And the clock turns back to reflect
On the years of grace
As those footsteps trace
For the last time out of the act
Well this way of life's recollection
The hallowed strip in the haze
The fabled men and the noonday sun
Are much more than just yarns of their days

'When an old cricketer leaves the crease', by Roy Harper

West Indian prototype: Constantine created the exciting blueprint for Caribbean cricket, but claimed many firsts in other areas of life and was acclaimed as much for the way he went about his business as for what he achieved

Contents

Preface

Despite the remarkable nature of Learie Constantine's life, in recent years his place in history appears to have come under threat.

In the popular British and West Indian consciousness he has lived on: many reasonably well-informed people have heard of his name, if nothing else, and are aware that he was a notable figure. Yet his star has undoubtedly been on the wane for some while.

Partly this is due to the passage of time, but that does not explain everything. Other prominent Caribbean figures, such as Constantine's contemporary CLR James, have had their reputations enhanced in many acres of print after their death. By contrast, very little has been written about Constantine since the immediate period after his demise, when his achievements and stature were still fresh enough in the mind to inspire two biographies. Since then, there has mostly been silence.

Mainly this is because academics and commentators, pre-occupied as they are with ideas and schools of thought, can find no real place for a practical man and ex-sportsman like Constantine who was not a man of letters and whose writings and political actions were essentially unassuming, even if highly influential. Because he was a populist non-intellectual, scandal-free and sensible, intent on finding down-to-earth solutions to the problems he had identified, his importance has tended to be under-rated and under-valued over time.

This book, using new material from personal papers and focusing as much upon Constantine's 'other' life as his cricketing existence, therefore hopes to help re-establish, in some way, Constantine's

IX

standing as one of the most important and extraordinary figures in black nationalism.

Many thanks to those who helped with its preparation, including Learie Constantine's daughter Gloria Valere; Gerada Holder at the Trinidad & Tobago Heritage Library; Professor Clem Seecharan; James Ferguson; Martin Bowen; Ken McIntyre and Martin Knight.

Introduction

Learie Constantine was a man of many firsts: first black Lord, first black sportsman of any real standing in Britain, first black governor of the BBC, to name but a few. He was a trailblazer not just in cricket, where he created the exciting blueprint for the West Indian game, but in the public life of both the Caribbean and Britain, where he played a significant role in fostering black nationalism and the cause of racial equality. Throughout his hugely eclectic life as sportsman, welfare worker, broadcaster, politician, author, diplomat, barrister and race relations pioneer, Constantine consistently pushed back many boundaries, arguing for change in whatever environment he functioned.

As one of the highest paid sportsmen in the world during the inter-war years, he raised cricket to new heights of excitement and prestige, while simultaneously agitating for an end to the 'colour bar' and class divisions in the game – both in the West Indies and elsewhere. As a welfare officer in Britain during the Second World War he played a vitally important part in championing the interests of black immigrants and easing racial tensions, while after the war his work in broadcasting, journalism and public life helped cement his place as the most popular and high profile black public figure in 20th-century British history. Through his unstinting support for the often controversial causes of Pan Africanism and racial equality, Constantine did as much as any individual to try to improve racial harmony in Britain and to bring about the Race Relations Act, even if his contribution has come to be downplayed or forgotten since his death in 1971. Constantine was not just one of cricket's best ever all-rounders; he was also one of the greatest all-rounders in the wider sense of the term, and one of the most well-known and influential of West Indians in the diaspora – as well as a role model for many West Indian immigrants.

In him were mirrored many of the struggles, tensions and aspirations that West Indians experienced during the 20th century. His life story was a reflection of the initial rejection, gradual acceptance and, in some areas, final acclaim, that was the lot of immigrants in Britain during the period.

His life also spanned and symbolized the wider Caribbean struggle from colonial dependency to independence – and the difficulties and unfulfilled expectations that followed. He had friendships with, and influence on, many of the main figures in that movement.

But Constantine was not just an important figure in the Caribbean and its diaspora; he was an immensely impressive human being; many dimensional, widely-loved, warm, honest, controversial, proud, and always engaging. In all areas, including his cricket, he was acclaimed as much for the way he went about his business as for what he achieved. As a man of firsts, many of his groundbreaking achievements will, by definition, never be repeated. Learie Constantine was, in any case, a one-off. His achievements will stand the test of time.

1 Early years

The exuberant nature of Trinidad travelled with Learie Constantine wherever he went throughout his life. Though he eventually spent many of his years away from the vibrant country of his birth, his happy childhood there was the bedrock on which he built his extraordinary life in the public eye. For many he embodied the gregarious charm and exotic grace of the place, and for his part he was always willing to talk about his roots. In his later years he harboured a deep-seated wish to return to Trinidad for good, and although illness and work prevented him from doing so, he carried the place in his heart to the end.

Constantine was born on 21 September 1901 in the small rural settlement of Petit Valley, close by the town of Diego Martin in the lush, mountainous, north western tip of Trinidad. He grew up in nearby St Anns, near Maraval, around four hilly miles to the north of the capital Port of Spain. The Trinidad of Constantine's birth was much more the sleepy Caribbean isle of popular imagination than the bustling place of one and a half million people it is today. Just seven miles off the coast of mainland South America, it was –

along with Barbados and Jamaica – one of the 'big three islands' in the British West Indies. But its mixed population of African, Indian and, to a lesser extent, Chinese and white European descent, was just 277,000, and the economy was still largely reliant on sugar and agriculture. There was significant poverty in the villages as well as in Port of Spain, and the country, under the dead hand of British rule, was struggling to cope with the social and economic fallout of slavery, abolished 60-odd years before.

Constantine's maternal grandfather, Ali Pascall, a Yoruba from West Africa, was born into slavery. His paternal great grandparents were among the last slaves to be brought over on the terrifying middle passage from Africa to the West Indies. Slavery was abolished on 1 August 1834, and lasted only 40 years in Trinidad – a relatively short period compared with its long dominance in other British West Indian countries such as Jamaica and Barbados. But the bitter experiences of the iniquitous plantation economy were still part of the collective memory of Constantine's family, if rarely talked about. Even the familial name was a reminder of a darker near-past, as it almost certainly belonged to a slave master, possibly the French landowner Jean Baptiste Constantin.

Although his family was never well-off, in relative terms, Constantine's childhood was a comfortable and idyllic one; much of it, from the age of around five, dedicated to running around in the local hills or playing cricket in the road with a barrel stave and oranges. The game had been brought to Trinidad relatively late, as the British had not taken control of the island from the Spanish until 1797, but just as in the rest of the British West Indies, cricket was the number one sport, shot through with a wider societal and cultural significance that could barely be comprehended outside its shores. In Trinidad, as Constantine recalled in middle age, 'cricket was almost worshipped, and ... the names of great English players were almost as legendary as those of the saints themselves'.

Constantine's father, Lebrun, who was born in Diego Martin in 1874, was a household name in Trinidad as a star batsman in the island team. He toured England with the very earliest West Indies squads of 1900 and 1906, scoring the first century (113) for the West Indies in England, two years before his first son Learie was born, against the MCC at Lord's. He named Learie (whose middle name was Nicholas) after a gregarious Irishman who had befriended him on his first tour. Lebrun was, according to the Trinidadian writer CLR James, who became a close acquaintance of Constantine junior in later life, 'the most loved and respected cricketer on the island', not just a superb batsman but a proficient bowler and wicketkeeper. He was the first black man to play for Trinidad in 1895, and one of the first to play for the West Indies in 1897. There was cricket on his mother's side too. Anaise Pascall's brother, Constantine's uncle Victor Pascall, also represented the West Indies as a slow left arm bowler, so there was no shortage of inspirational cricketing talent in the blood – or wise heads to nurture it.

The Constantine family, like Trinidad in general, was cricket mad. The patriarchal Lebrun, 'Old Pa' or 'Old Cons' as he was popularly known, had constructed a matting wicket – known locally as 'the Constantine pitch' – in the family's backyard when they moved, when Constantine was about six, to St Anns. On this the whole tribe of Constantines – Learie, his three younger brothers, Osmund, Rodney and Elias, sister Leonora, mother and father – would play and practise, often daily until it was dark. Old Cons was the supportive but stern coach, demanding the highest standards and often bowling at full pace, insisting that the game should be played for the joy of it first and for the technical niceties second. Constantine always maintained that his mother (sometimes known as 'Anna') could keep wicket not far short of international standard, and that his sister had as much talent in her early days as he did. Rodney died in his twenties, but Osmund, who became a building contractor in later life, was a good wicketkeeper – and Elias went on to represent Trinidad. Constantine remembered that they were happy in those early matches 'to a degree that seems only really attainable under the blazing West Indian sun'.

While he taught all the nuances of the game, Old Cons' particular obsession was with the value of good fielding – one of his own strong points – and he would involve children and wife in lengthy catching practice. 'We were kept at it every spare moment of daylight,' Constantine would recall later. 'My father knew the dictum that genius is one-tenth inspiration and nine-tenths perspiration.' He and Elias would practise their catching by throwing each other the crockery as they washed up, or by hurling open knives at each other, and his father's insistence on the virtues of catching and throwing, rather unusual at the time, was at least partly responsible for his son's legendary fielding prowess, which became a cornerstone of his game in later life. 'He was a martinet,' recalled Constantine. 'If one ball got away from you and then another ... then he would give you a rap on the head.'

Both parents were hard taskmasters in all areas, not just cricket. They laid down a strong moral code – Constantine was once beaten by his mother for 'stealing' an egg he found lying in a ditch – but by Constantine's own account they were fair and loving within the harsh strictures of the day, emphasizing decency and good manners at all times. The warmth of his family counted for a lot, and gave him strength. 'A happy childhood is one of the greatest defences a man can have against the world,' he said later. He often claimed that the beloved cricketing sessions in the backyard and the strong sense of values that surrounded them 'served as a cushion, I am sure, for the sterner life which was ahead for all of us'.

Although his early years were blissfully ignorant of one constant aspect of that later and sterner life – racial prejudice – there was an early indication of things to come when, aged five, he was urgently hustled into the house by his mother as a white estate owner rode recklessly by on his horse. The man, he was told, would happily have ridden over any nigger children if they had got anywhere near his path. The incident always stayed in his mind as a neat summary of what he later encountered beyond the safe confines of the family home.

Although Constantine was a bright and conscientious pupil at the St Anns Government School in Port of Spain until he was around 12, then at the St Anns Roman Catholic School from 1914 to 1917, he was never an outstanding or especially enthusiastic scholar. His parents urged him to make the most of what was only a basic education, but he was not proficient enough to get one of the highly-prized scholarships that would have set him on course for better things than his father's job as a cocoa estate overseer.

While he dreamed of a solid berth in the professions – perhaps, at the time, more at the behest of parental ambitions than through any of his own – the reality was that Constantine's social standing made the realization of that dream nearly impossible. He may have come from cricketing royalty, but his lineage outside the game was anything but regal. Old Cons' cricketing career brought him little if any money, and though he worked for a relatively liberal boss in a job that was often reserved for white men, he was not well rewarded for his work. His 25-year career as an international batsman had to be fitted around work commitments, and on the West Indies tour to England in 1906 he was famously left behind in Trinidad because he couldn't afford the passage. When a local white merchant, Michael Maillard, found out – on the day the squad set sail – he hastily raised the cash to pay for Old Cons' trip, and the player was sent out to meet the boat by fast launch with new kit and clothes.

Old Cons and his son were dark skinned, in a colony where skin tones mattered. Neither father nor son had the vote: only around one in 20 adults – almost all white or near-white – had that privilege. It would have been abundantly clear to the young boy that while Old Cons was one of the most admired and well recognized people in Trinidad, this counted for very little in social terms, where he was firmly entrenched as a member of the black lower middle class.

When he ended his elementary education at age 15 in 1917, too young to be called up to fight in the West Indies Regiment in the remote First World War, Constantine found work as a law clerk in the legal firm of Jonathan Ryan in Port of Spain, nurturing the hope – encouraged by his father – that he might be able to train to enter the legal profession. Ryan was a decent employer, and Constantine, who prepared summonses, took statements and typed up notes, eventually moved up to become chief clerk. But the pay was poor, and even if he could have ground his way through the ten years of necessary studying, solicitors' jobs were rarely if ever open to dark skinned people in the Trinidad of the early 1900s.

In truth, while he was probably as determined as he ever was in those days to break out of the social straitjacket imposed on him, Constantine was really more engaged by sporting endeavours, which had been nurtured not just in his backyard but also at his Catholic school. There he captained the team and received coaching from the headmaster, Andrew De Four, whose influence on his game in those early days was second only to Constantine's father.

In parallel to his work in the solicitor's office, which at least had the benefit of an early-finishing time that allowed him to practise cricket, he began to develop a cricketing career under the guiding influence and unforgiving standards of his father and his uncle Victor. James described the young Constantine as a 'thickset, rather slow boy' when he first saw him at the age of nine in 1911, but that condition didn't last for long. Very soon Constantine was establishing himself in Trinidad as a player of quite exceptional sharpness and guile – particularly in the field. A hard-hitting right-handed all rounder who adopted his father's all-action batting style, he had, by the age of 15, become a very promising medium-fast bowler, and was already an exceptional fielder, fearlessly hurling himself at the ball and showing incredible powers of anticipation. For a time Old Cons had forbidden the young Constantine from entering top line club cricket in Trinidad on the grounds that while he was certainly good enough to enter the fray, too early an exposure to the wily ways of the island's top cricketers might reduce his confidence and spoil his talent. But when he did move into the main arena he made an immediate impact.

Constantine honed his emerging talent at Shannon Cricket Club, for whom he first played in 1916 when the club was known as Victoria. As James so eloquently described in his classic book

Beyond a Boundary, Trinidadian cricket of the era was rigidly divided on colour and class lines, with the white and wealthy Queen's Park Club, which played at the island's best appointed ground, the beautiful Queen's Park Oval in Port of Spain, firmly at the top of the hierarchy. As James noted, Constantine would have been more easily elected to the MCC – the conservative bastion of English cricket – than to play for Queen's Park. Shannon was the club of the black lower middle classes and would have been the place that he naturally drifted to, even if his father hadn't happened to be the captain. Like many of the other major teams, including Stingo (the top team of the black lower classes) and Maple (the premier club for the light-skinned middle classes), Shannon played on the rough grounds of the Savannah: a huge, picturesque open space in Port of Spain big enough to hold dozens of cricket pitches, most with a single large tree that acted as changing room, place of shade and clubhouse.

Trinidad's blazing hot weather allowed cricket to be played eight months of the year, and the crowds at Shannon matches were often large. Conditions were not ideal, with coconut matting rather than grass wickets and roughly mown outfields, but Shannon was the best club in the country, provider of many of Trinidad's international cricketers and a perfect cradle of the game for Constantine to learn his trade.

Above all, Shannon played with immense determination, thought and application – characteristics that were to mark Constantine out in his later days on the international stage, not just in cricket but in other spheres of life. James recalled that the 'spirit and restlessness' of the side set it apart from all others. 'It was not mere skill,' he remembered, 'they played as if they knew that their club represented the great mass of black people on the island. By their play they said: "Here on the cricket field, if nowhere else, all in the island are equal – and we are the best men in the island." No Australian team could teach them anything in relentless concentration. They missed few catches and looked upon one of their number who committed such a crime as a potential fifth columnist.' Cricket was a serious business for Shannon, and although from the start Constantine was nearly always a genial presence on the field, he had the inner steel required of all who turned out for the club. On one occasion he had become seriously ill during the course of a match (games were played over two weekends, with two innings per side), but with his side in trouble at eight wickets down, he arrived at the ground and crawled to the wicket in his daytime shoes and clothes. He was so weak he hardly had the strength to wield his bat, and was out first ball. But the tough standards set by Old Cons and Uncle Victor, also a player at Shannon, would have allowed nothing else but that he made the effort.

James, who was not a Shannon player, recounted how many years later, when both he and Constantine were fielding in a low key friendly match in England, an uppish shot came in James's direction. 'Not one county cricketer in three could possibly have got to it, and in any case a friendly is a friendly. Or so I thought, until I heard a savage shout from Constantine, who had bowled the ball. "Get to it!" I recognized the note. It was one Shannon player calling to another.'

It is difficult to underestimate the importance of that Shannon ethos in Constantine's life. What he found at the club was not just an extension of the discipline and focus he was forced to live by in his life at home, but a road map for the rest of his existence – a chart that pointed the way to honest endeavour, discipline, principled behaviour, and a constant striving to make the best of one's abilities. When he later went to places where this ethos did not exist, or was cast aside, he became deeply frustrated. 'No one could appear to play more gaily, more spontaneously, more attractively than Constantine, [yet] in reality he was a cricketer of concentrated passion, irked during all his big cricket life by the absence of what he found when he played with Shannon,' said James.

The young player found out pretty soon that outside the confines of Shannon, factors other than passion and application were more important in the cricketing world. West Indies cricket was not a meritocracy – anything but – and while Constantine himself was soon noticed as a potential international player, others with the wrong skin colour and lesser parentage found themselves strangely overlooked for honours while a succession of inferior white or light skinned players took their places. All of this deeply affected Constantine, as it did many others. By the 1920s he was privately agitating against the custom that the West Indies captain should always be a white man, arguing, at least to his friends and black cricketing colleagues, that it was time for radical change. Playing for Shannon and watching racism at work in cricket politicized him from an early point.

Ironically, however, it was partly as a result of the support of two white men that Constantine progressed so quickly from Shannon to represent Trinidad and then the West Indies. At the age of 19 he was chosen to play for Trinidad in the 1921 inter-colonial tournament, the annual triangular competition against Barbados and British Guiana. His passage into first class cricket had been eased by his father, who had selflessly decided not to put himself forward for Trinidad in 1921 in the private hope that his son would take his place. But he was selected chiefly at the behest of Major Bertie Harrigan, the white Trinidad captain, who saw something in the wiry, muscular lad that he wanted to encourage.

Constantine made an inauspicious start to his first class career when, to his horror and Harrigan's anger, a newspaper misprint of the start time led him to turn up late for his debut game against British Guiana at the Queen's Park Oval. He described it as 'one of the nastiest shocks I ever had in my life' and he missed out on the match as a result, forced to sit, head in hands, on the sidelines. On his eventual first class debut, against Barbados in the same competition, he did nothing of great note, scoring 0 and 24, although he did take two wickets for 44 runs off 21 overs and held a good catch at slip.

First class games in the West Indies were few and far between in those days, and it wasn't until a year later that he got the chance to represent Trinidad in their next match, when he went away on his first trip abroad to play against British Guiana in 1922. Again there was little to write home about with bat or ball, but his major impact came in the field when, quite by chance, he was moved from his position in the slips to cover point. On the beautiful outfield at Georgetown he established himself from that day on as a truly exceptional fielder in the covers. More or less on the basis of his fielding alone, he was again selected for Trinidad in the next inter-colonial tournament match against Barbados, along with his 48-year-old father, who was playing his last game. It was one of the few instances of a father and son appearing together in a first class game, and for good measure Uncle Victor also took the field. It was a match the family cherished.

Despite Constantine's undistinguished start, Harold Austin, the white skipper of Barbados and West Indies, took him under his wing, championing his cause and picking him for the 1923 West Indies tour to England with just three first class matches under his belt. It was a bold decision given that a handful of others, including the Trinidadian-born Barbados fast bowler Herman Griffith, had a better case for inclusion. Constantine was by no means the finished article, but he was determined to make a mark. Though he was diligent in his law clerk role, he was getting nowhere fast, and shortly before his inclusion in the tour party he had left Jonathan Ryan in 1922 to join Llewellyn Roberts, a larger solicitor's practice in Port of Spain that would give him a greater breadth of experience and, perhaps, better prospects. However, he had to work longer and more inconvenient hours, restricting his time for cricket practice. When he received the news that he had been picked to tour England, he resigned his job. It was a tough decision to make given that he would be returning to unemployment – and he knew he wouldn't make his fortune from the tour. With a weekly allowance of only 30 shillings, those of his fellow tourists who smoked could hardly afford even to buy cigarettes while they were away. But Constantine was 20 years old and prepared to take the risk. Besides, 'to go to England to play cricket was at that time my idea of heaven on earth', he said.

Constantine, known affectionately throughout his cricketing life as 'Connie', set off on the England tour in April 1923, landing in Bristol on the SS *Intaba* and returning in September. Like many West Indians who followed him on similar journeys as immigrants 40 and 50 years later, his experience of the cold grey reality of the mother country hardly lived up to the rosy picture painted for him by the colonial authorities throughout his schooldays. Although, typically for a man who was always interested in his surroundings, he found the experience fascinating and the ocean voyage a joy, the culture shock was considerable. 'I recall miserable journeys in freezing rain, from one damp hotel to another; dressing rooms with their own private chills laid on, and afternoons in the field when it was impossible to pay attention because one kept thinking about overcoats,' he said later. Although Constantine marvelled at the orderly English countryside with its 'prim green fields and well arranged trees', he railed at the boredom of closed-up English Sundays, was troubled by the national reserve, found himself unable to distinguish one Englishman from the next, and was blighted by the bitter cold of the especially bad summer of that year. At first he put the English reticence down to 'the colour bar', but by the end of the tour had come to the conclusion that 'on the whole [race] makes less difference in England than in the West Indies'.

In 1923 the West Indies were still a fledgling national side, a point of interest in England for their novelty value (not least for the racial mix of the team) but not expected to trouble many of the first class county sides and certainly not deemed good enough to merit any Test matches against the national team. But the tourists, captained by Austin and with the white Barbadian batsman George Challenor as its brightest star, did much to change that perception. They won six and lost only seven of 21 first class matches over the six months, and went some way to laying the foundations for West Indies to be granted official Test status in 1928.

Foreign tours were very much a commercial enterprise in this era. Quite apart from the pride involved, it was important that the tourists put on a decent show to maintain interest and draw in the crowds. Challenor was a star, but Constantine's exciting brand of cricket was also good for the box office, and although he scored only 425 runs and took a modest 37 wickets on the tour, he played

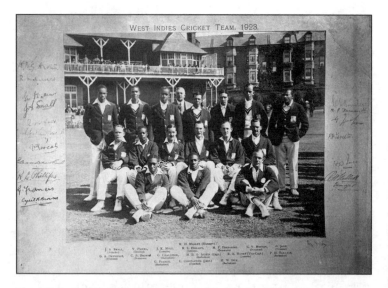

WEST INDIES CRICKET TEAM, 1923.

R. H. Mallet (Manager)

J. A. Small   V. Pascal   J. K. Holt   R. L. Phillips   M. P. Fernandes   C. V. Hunter   G. John
(Trinidad)   (Trinidad)   (Jamaica)   (Jamaica)   (Demerara)   (Demerara)   (Trinidad)

G. A. Dewhurst   C. R. Browne   G. Challenor   H. B. G. Austin (Capt.)   R. K. Nunes (Vice-Capt.)   P. H. Tarilton
(Trinidad)   (Demerara)   (Barbados)   (Barbados)   (Jamaica)   (Barbados)

G. Francis   L. Constantine (Asst.)   H. W. Ince
(Barbados)   (Trinidad)   (Barbados)

Trailblazers: the 1923 West Indies touring team, with Constantine centre of the front row

no less a role in marketing the West Indies to the British public than Challenor. The explosive nature of his batting, bowling and cover point fielding impressed the English spectators, who had never seen anything like him before. The grand old man of cricket, Pelham Warner, called him 'the finest fielder in the world', and the public and press agreed. 'In the deep he picked up while going like a sprinter, and threw with explosive accuracy,' said the cricketers' bible *Wisden*. 'Close to the wicket he was fearless and quick; wherever he was posted he amazed everyone by his speed and certainty in making catches which seemed far beyond reach. His movement was so joyously fluid and, at need, acrobatic, that he might have been made of springs and rubber.'

Although Constantine had natural fielding talent, he did not arrive at this by accident. The author AM Clarke reported that the young cricketer spent countless hours teaching himself the art of balance by bending down to pick up an object from the floor, progressively placing himself further away from it until he had to balance on one foot to reach it, snatching it before he fell over. His bowling, at first or second change, and his batting, in the lower order, were less exceptional and more erratic, but an occasional aggressive outburst with the ball or bat caught the imagination. More than that, Constantine had a presence and certain dignity about him that endeared him to the crowds. 'His appearance was striking: his big, loose frame around middle height, the bold sculpture of his face, the black lustrous eyes, direct and intense, the long dominating nose, the wide sympathetic yet firm mouth, and the strong chin, all conveyed an irresistible impression of decisiveness and strength,' said Clarke.

There was rarely a dull moment while the new star was at the crease, and he loved to hit sixes. *Wisden* described his batting, 'which depended considerably upon the eye', as 'sometimes unorthodox to the point of spontaneous invention' and noted that 'on his day it was virtually impossible to bowl at him'. Though relatively short for a fast bowler at no more than five feet eleven, he was lithe, 'stocky but long armed', and bowled 'with a bounding run, a high, smooth action and considerable pace'. Jack Hobbs, the greatest English batsmen of all time, was sufficiently impressed by Constantine's performances on that tour to give the young player special instruction, and he was also judged an exceptional talent by the England players Patsy Hendren and Herbert Sutcliffe. The tour of 1923 confirmed Constantine as one of the most gifted and entertaining all-rounders of the day.

Constantine was happy to take the acclaim back with him to the West Indies, but when he docked in Port of Spain, his exploits in England counted for little when it came to making a living. Although Constantine was feted by the black populace, his off the field status had hardly changed for the better. Now unemployed, he eventually found a temporary post as a civil servant in the registrar's office of the supreme court, followed by another temporary position in the education department, where he busied himself with typing, filing and general administration work. But both jobs were filled by other, lighter-skinned applicants when the time came to find a permanent holder. During 1924 and 1925 Constantine was in and out of work and strapped for cash, often relying on his family to keep the wolf from the door and by now living with his parents in the village of Arouca, about 10 miles east of Port of Spain, where his father had taken on a government job as a ward officer. Thoughts of the 1923 tour kept him going. 'On that visit he learnt much that he never forgot, by no means all of it about cricket: and he recognised the game as his only possible ladder to the kind of life he wanted,' observed *Wisden*.

Constantine continued to play for Shannon, for whom he hit a brilliant 167 not out against Queen's Park in 1924, and he turned out for Trinidad in the inter-colonial tournaments of 1924 and 1925 against Barbados and British Guiana, making respectable totals against Barbados at Bridgetown (38) in 1924 and in Port of Spain (36) the following year. In the winter of 1925/6, at the insistence of Austin, he also got the chance to play four games – two for Trinidad and two for a West Indies XI – against a visiting MCC touring team. As was the case for much of his career, it was not the number of runs or wickets he got in these matches, but the wholehearted, exciting way in which he took them that caught everyone's eye. His exuberance also embroiled him in a brief controversy over the use of short pitched bowling when, in retaliation for some hostile stuff directed by the MCC bowlers at the West Indies skipper Austin, now in his late 40s, Constantine decided to reciprocate with intimidating bowling at the rather shaky MCC skipper, the honourable FSG Calthorpe. It was indicative of Constantine's bold spirit and unflinching belief in equality that he even thought of targeting such a lofty establishment figure. James and some of his friends, watching at the Queen's Park Oval, viewed things differently and urgently sought Constantine in the dressing room at the interval. 'I was scared stiff,' reported James later. 'Two or three of us went to Constantine. "Stop it, Learie!" we told him. He replied: "What's wrong with you? It's cricket." I told him bluntly: "Do not bump the ball at that man. He is the MCC captain, the captain of an English county and an English aristocrat. The bowling is obviously too fast for him and if you hit him and knock him down there will be a hell of a row and we don't want to see you in any such mess. Stop it!" He was rebellious, but we were adamant. He saw what we were driving at, finally agreed, and loyally kept the ball out of harm's way.' While the incident may have revealed some young naivety, it was also an early and revealing insight into Constantine's character. At heart he was a passionate, rebellious man who railed against the iniquitous status quo but, in the final analysis, was prepared to rein in his tempestuous side in the hope that a more measured approach would reap rewards.

Despite the stir he invariably caused whenever he stepped on to a cricket field, Constantine essentially underachieved in the immediate period after coming back from the 1923 tour. Coupled with his work-related disappointments, this began to prompt him to think more seriously about his future. Although he had worked hard in his law clerk jobs and then in his temporary civil servant posts, Constantine's chances of making significant progress were, in his own words, 'unrealizable', partly because of his skin colour and partly, as he later conceded, because work interfered with his love of cricket. In the cricketing backwater of Trinidad, where there was no prospect of making a living out of the game and he could expect no more than three or four first class games a year, his sporting abilities were also going to waste. Constantine was gradually coming to the conclusion that if he was to make the most of himself, then he would have to leave behind his hopes of career progression and depart the island, 'throwing away eight years of hard labour so as to claim the right to live instead of exist'.

Constantine eventually got himself a new administrative job as an £8 a month clerk in the by-now burgeoning Trinidad oilfields, working for a company called Trinidad Leaseholds. The firm was run by HCW Johnson, a sympathetic white South African who, as an outsider in the country, felt less constrained by hide-bound employment conventions. Nonetheless the job, which took Constantine down to the south of the island to work in the small town of Fyzabad near the island's second city of San Fernando, was still one strictly limited in its prospects. In those early days in the oilfields of Trinidad, as the historian and Jamaican prime minister Michael Manley noted in his history of West Indies cricket, the administrative staff were divided into two groups: one white and very light skinned and the other dark, working to the unwritten rule that 'beyond a certain limit, dark could not aspire'. But at least Constantine's new employer was generous with time off, allowing the young cricketer leave on half pay whenever he needed to play representative matches. He turned out for the company on Saturdays, which reduced his opportunity to play for Shannon, and he got himself fitter than ever by playing football for the island's Forest Reserve team, as well as representing the company as a sprinter, winning several cups in the process. He was so quick over 100 yards that he had even beaten Ben Sealey, the Trinidadian champion at that distance. Initially his job often required Constantine to work long hours. But in 1927, after he complained about his workload, he was transferred to Pointe-à-Pierre, a small town slightly further north of Fyzabad, where a new environment allowed him more time to practise cricket. He married his long time sweetheart Norma Cox, whom he had first met in Port of Spain six years earlier, on 25 July 1927 and in April 1928 they had their only child Gloria. Norma, a pretty and intelligent city girl whose chemist father had died when she was seven, had by her own estimation 'come a very poor second to the cricket' during their courtship, and at one stage had given him an ultimatum to choose between her or the game. Constantine had begged her to 'please let it be you *and* cricket – I don't want to give up either'. So disarming was his request that she resolved to take a much keener interest in his sporting exploits from that point onwards. Norma had stuck by him during the recent hard times, and Constantine's new family responsibilities only served to re-emphasize to him the importance of somehow engineering a more secure future. For some time now the young man had been working on a plan to make the most of his cricketing talents, and the more relaxed atmosphere of the oilfields had allowed him to begin to put it into force. 'I did some hard thinking, and not only some thinking, but some acting too,' he said. 'I set to work at my cricket.'

Constantine's plan was focused around the forthcoming 1928 tour of West Indies to England, where he aimed to make such a mark that he would be offered a job as a professional in one of the Lancashire or Yorkshire leagues, which at the time were among the highest paying in the game. For much of his early career Constantine had made his name chiefly as an outstanding fielder. Although he had great talent as a batsman and bowler, he rarely displayed it for long periods or on a regular basis, and was often accused even by his most enthusiastic supporters of coasting. He was not yet a really fast bowler, even though his great athleticism suggested he could be, and while he was technically more superior as a batsman than many of his international peers, he was carefree, giving his wicket away too easily. 'We used to beg him to settle down and bat,' said James. 'All of us were looking for him to do great things, but he simply wouldn't settle down.' However, as Constantine started to realize from 1923 onwards that cricket might be his only salvation, he began to see their point of view, admitting to himself that while he had made a few big scores, 'to most cricketers in the West Indies I was only a swiper'. He resolved to do better. Over the five years up to 1928, and particularly after the moderate personal results of 1926 against the touring MCC, Constantine began to ally application to his great talent. He realized that if he wanted to be a consistently fast bowler he would have to give up his all action position at cover point, which would drain him of energy between overs. But he was determined to maintain his status as the world's greatest fielder, and to put huge efforts into becoming a superb catcher closer to the bat at slip, where he would not have to run around so much. He had always been a great observer of the intricacies of cricket, and largely through self tuition and self-discipline, shaped by the Shannon ethos and his intrinsic love of the game, he pulled himself up to a new level. He also instigated a tough

Make a break: Constantine (left) on the 1928 West Indies tour of England with fellow tourist Wilton St Hill

fitness regime, getting up at dawn to run, lifting weights and using chest expanders.

The effect was not immediate – he was again modest in first class matches for Trinidad in 1927 – but by the time he came to play two crucial West Indies trial matches against Barbados in January 1928 he was bowling with more pace and batting with more application than he had ever done before, scoring a quickfire 63 in one match and taking five for 32 in another. Given his average performances in first class matches over the previous two years, he could not have complained if he had been left out of the squad to tour England that year. But the new dynamism he revealed at the trial matches was enough to gain him selection. Trinidad Leaseholds put him on half pay and he went to England, leaving Norma and daughter behind. While the 1923 tour had been an adventure, this time Constantine had a specific mission: to play so well and to be so entertaining that he would be asked to come back to England in some professional capacity. 'I knew I could not keep up both cricket and business, and I did not want to do as so many other West Indians had done – be forced into a position where I did neither thing to the best of my ability,' he said. This time England would be his escape – and this time he had not stinted on the preparation. 'When I landed in England I was as fit a man as I have ever been in my life,' he declared.

2 Nelson: a model professional

Constantine wanted to get ahead – and the 1928 tour was his chance. Had he been able to make a good living in Trinidad playing cricket, or for that matter practising law, then it is likely he would have stayed and taken his chances. But, approaching the age of 27 and with the talent at his disposal, he felt he deserved more. He was a self-improver, as the recent work on his game had showed, and he was not going to settle for his father's life of financially unrewarded renown. Unlike most of the white players in the West Indian cricketing world, he had neither the private income nor the social standing to be able to play cricket purely for fun. James believed that 'if Constantine had had not only honour but a little profit in his own country he never would have settled abroad', further observing that 'had his skin been white like George Challenor's, or even light, he would have been able to choose a life at home'. In the final analysis, 'he revolted against the revolting contrast between his first-class status as a cricketer and his third-class status as a man'. Tracking a new course in England appeared to be the only attractive option available to him.

The 1928 tour, then, was not just a trip to England for Constantine – it was the most crucial passage of his life. Despite his charismatic presence in West Indian cricket, he had played just 36 first class matches up to that point, and in those he had shone only intermittently. He needed to show himself in the international shop window. Thanks to the hard work that he had put in before coming to England in April 1928, he was now not only a hard-hitting, high-octane batsman and the world's best fielder, nicknamed 'electric heels', but as fast a bowler as anyone in the world.

As a consequence, Constantine's performances in 1928 were all that he had hoped for. He had made a mark when he toured England in 1923, but this time he jumped right into fortune and fame, establishing himself as the most exciting cricketer of his era. In the first tour game against Derbyshire, Constantine went in to bat with his team having only two wickets in hand and needing 40 more runs to win. To the delight of the crowd he blasted virtually all of them himself in a flurry of boundaries. 'I ought to have been careful but I did not feel careful,' he said later. 'I had been watching the bowling and knew that the Lord had given it into mine hand.' Things had started well, and he followed up with a century against Essex. But it was the fourth match of the tour against Middlesex in June, at Lord's, the fabled headquarters of the game, that proved to be the defining moment for Constantine. Having torn a muscle in the previous game against Surrey (in which he scored 50 and 60 not out) he was advised by the team doctor to rest for at least ten days. The first recognized official Test matches between England and West Indies were to follow shortly, and he should have put his feet up. But mindful that the tour was looking as if it might fail to cover its costs, and aware that after a less than convincing team start to the summer, another defeat against a county side would reduce interest in the forthcoming first Test, Constantine was urged by the team manager, RH Mallett, to consider playing. 'You are our draw card, Cons,' he said. 'If you drop out we shan't do much business. But you must decide yourself. I don't want you to harm yourself.'

Constantine decided to take the risk, and he was well rewarded for his bravery. The injury prevented him from bowling more than a few overs in the first innings, and Middlesex batted with ease, posting the formidable total of 352 for six declared. The visitors, in reply, had slumped to an embarrassing 79 for five by the time Constantine walked out at number seven, and they were facing the ignominy of an innings defeat. Though in great pain, he thrashed 50 in 18 minutes – still one of the fastest half-centuries ever recorded in first class cricket – and, going on to score a rumbustuous 86 out of 107 in under an hour, helped West Indies to a respectable 230, which put them back in the match. Now thoroughly fired up, Constantine decided to bowl in Middlesex's second innings – as fast as he could. Despite his injury, and drawing on all the inner reserves and hard work he had put together in Trinidad over the past five years, he tore in at great speed to rip Middlesex apart, finishing with seven wickets for 57 – including a devastating spell of six wickets for just 11 runs off 39 balls. Middlesex had made only 136 this time, but that still left the fragile West Indies needing 259 to win in their second innings. Again they proved well short of the task, and this time Constantine came in at 121 for five. Staring straight down the barrel of the gun, he scored a tumultuous 103 in an hour that snatched victory by three wickets and earned him a standing ovation – his second of the match. One journalist reported that the normally restrained members in the pavilion,

The original one day cricketer: Constantine's all action batting style set league cricket alight

forgetting that their own team had lost, 'stood bare headed, hoarse from cheering' as he came back to the pavilion, while 'the boys who sold match cards, the men who minded the gate, the ground staff at their posts, all to a man rushed to the edge of the field to join the crowd who clapped the hero every yard of his way home'. It was batting and bowling of incredibly destructive force: the

Middlesex fielder Jack Hearne was hit so hard on the hand by one Constantine shot that he was out with a broken finger for the rest of the summer. It was also one of the great all round performances of all time, still regarded by cricket historians as such. According to the academic and historian Angus Calder, the great batsman Denis Compton, who joined Middlesex as a teenager a few years later, 'found the old pros in the dressing room still talking with awe' about Constantine's innings as the best they had ever seen. It was the cricketing sensation of the season. The *Trinidad Guardian* published a special issue to mark the achievement, and wherever he went in the West Indies for years afterwards, he was asked about that match. It is no exaggeration to say that Constantine's performance at Lord's was the most important of his career, for it not only put him firmly on the cricketing map, it led directly to an offer to play as a professional with the Lancashire League club Nelson. Within two months of arriving in England he had already achieved his goal. Given all that was to follow, it was the most significant turning point in his life.

Lord's apart, it was a golden and heroic summer for Constantine, who was really the only West Indies success story of the tour. Although he and his colleagues performed below par in the first three officially recognized Test matches between England and the West Indies that season, which they lost each by an innings, Constantine finished the tour as the leading run scorer with 1381 runs (average 34.52), leading wicket taker with 107 wickets (22.95), and leading fielder with 29 catches. He also became the first West Indian to claim a wicket in a Test match, when he dismissed Charles Hallows at Lord's, finishing with four for 82. Jack Hobbs declared that Constantine's first few overs against him in that match were as quick as anything he had ever faced in his life, and the new verve in his bowling was a revelation. Apart from the Middlesex game he also performed heroics against Northamptonshire later in the tour, taking 13 wickets in the match, including a second innings hat trick, and hitting 107 in 90 minutes. Again he had gone into the game carrying an injury, and at the close of play he had to be carried to his hotel room by his team mates. *Wisden* announced that Constantine was 'in public esteem quite the most successful member of the party', while the *Who's Who of Cricketers* identified him as 'the outstanding figure of the visit'.

What caught the public imagination so firmly was not just the deeds, however, but the manner of them. Here at last was a fully fledged, identifiably West Indian style of play – dramatic, unfettered, full of fun and aggression. The emotional impact this had in the England of the 1920s, where mannered, gentlemanly strokeplay or dogged hard edged professionalism had become the order of the day, should not be underestimated. Constantine was a breath of fresh air. His innings were dramatic and exhilarating, his bowling hostile and combative, and his fielding quite simply the best there had ever been. 'Those who saw him in his prime do not expect to be contradicted when they tell you that he was one of the great outfielders of all time, panther-quick, sure handed and with an arm that could rifle the ball into the wicketkeeper's gloves like a bullet, even from the deepest boundary,' said Manley. What's more, Constantine had grown in confidence and maturity since the last time he appeared in England, when he had been rather shy. By his own account, he made 'dozens of good friends' among English cricketers this time round, and this allowed his natural exuberance to come to the fore. On the pitch he had a cheeky and combative demeanour but, above all, a joyous attitude to the game that was infectious. Spectators particularly loved his little tricks and party pieces, the most popular of which he used to perform as he was walking back towards his bowling mark. A complicit fielder, returning the ball, would hurl it straight at Constantine's spine while he was looking in the opposite direction, only for Constantine to flick his hand behind his back, at the last possible moment, to catch the ball clean between his shoulder blades – while still not looking. He would also often fool the crowd by taking a breathtakingly quick slip catch, only to pocket the ball almost in the same movement and then turn away as if watching the ball speeding to the boundary.

Constantine, in short, had laid down the template for the black West Indian cricketer – fast bowler, hard-hitting batsman and electric fielder. Manley made the point by comparing him with Challenor, who, though 40 years old in 1928, played with Constantine on that tour. 'One was the product of the white upper classes of Barbados. Inevitably he was a batsman, well coached, with a good eye and sound technique. He was a great driver of the ball, a virtue which he shared with every great English batsman in history. By contrast, Constantine was a black Trinidadian. It was symbolic, if not quite socially inevitable, that Constantine would be a bowler and Challenor a batsman. It was equally a product of the times that Constantine would bat like a man inspired, his every stroke owing more to energy than calculation, more to instinct than to teaching.'

If Constantine's expressive game was later to translate, for some, into the stereotype of 'calypso cricket' – carrying with it the tacit implication that it contained little thought or discipline – then that was no fault of Constantine, but the fault of the stereotype. Constantine was aware of the perceptions that tied themselves to his play, and to that of other West Indians who followed in his wake, but he was happy to play the way he did, for he felt it was a natural expression of his self. 'It has always been a legitimate target for the critics, this business of our temperaments,' he said. 'But personally I like to *play* cricket, and find the wooden-faced stance rather chilling.'

Of course many West Indian cricketers who followed Constantine played nothing like him. But he put down a marker for the joyful spirit in which West Indian cricket has often been framed. He also laid a foundation stone for the greatness of West Indies cricketers to follow, from Sobers to Richards to Lara. The separate identity that Constantine coined for West Indies, as much as anything, allowed the team to plant a foot in international cricket during that 1928 summer, despite poor showings in the three Tests. But quite apart from the influence he had on West Indies' long term future, Constantine's 1928 exploits had a dramatic impact on his own circumstances.

At the end of the England tour, safe in the knowledge that he had signed a three-year professional contract with Nelson in September, he returned home to his family, Trinidad and a winter with Shannon. During the inter-colonial tournament he continued his good form, taking nine wickets against British Guiana in January 1929 and then scoring 133 against Barbados (the highest first class score of his career), before taking seven wickets in the game to win the tournament for Trinidad to enhance his hero status on the island.

When the winter was up, he and Norma had a new life to go to in England. Virtually on the basis of his Middlesex performance alone, Nelson had engaged Constantine up to the end of the 1931 season on pay of £500 a season in weekly payments of £25 plus travelling expenses for him and Norma from Trinidad and up to

£100 per season in bonuses – a guinea for every 50 he scored and the same amount for every five wickets. Overnight he had become one of the highest paid sportsmen in Britain.

The 14-club Lancashire League was a vibrant and successful entity by 1929. Nelson had 1500 members paying up to £3 a year in membership fees, and regularly attracted gates of 8,000 out of a population of only 40,000 – far in excess of attendances at many county matches. Gate takings alone could raise £200 a match. Constantine was well rewarded as a result, and for the first time in his life had the chance to become comfortably well off.

Nelson were actually in debt to the tune of almost £3,000 when Constantine joined them, but they were clear into profit within three years, almost entirely because of the pulling power of their professional. He made them the richest club in the League. But Constantine was also a boon to the League in general. Such was his drawing power that he not only increased Nelson's home gates dramatically (up to 14,000 on occasion) but those of all the other teams who played in the competition. While there were other professionals who could attract attention, gate receipts often went up by more than £100 for a game in which Constantine was playing, and League historians have estimated that between 1929 and 1933, when Constantine first hit the scene, receipts in matches involving Nelson accounted for three quarters of all the League's gate money, boosting attendances by something like 50,000 a year across the board. When he renewed his three-year contract in 1931, Constantine's salary went up to £650 a year, and when in 1934 there were attempts to lure him to another league for £1,100, all the other Lancashire League teams, mindful of the potential drop in revenues, contributed money to help Nelson keep him. They also collectively paid £250 into a fund set up for his benefit year in 1935, which raised around £500 overall. These levels of earnings – for what was effectively a summer job – put Constantine's pay, if not his overall income, streets ahead of the average professional footballer – who was restricted by the maximum wage – and well above even the top professional cricketer on the county and Test circuit. In all probability it also outstripped the regular earnings even of the top jockeys or boxers of the day. Given the opacity of sporting accounts in those days, there is no sure way of telling that Constantine really was the best-paid professional sportsman of 1930s Britain. But the consensus seems to be that he probably was. Constantine, for one, was convinced of the fact, advertising it in print. Whatever the case, he was earning the equivalent of a doctor's yearly salary in just a few months, was probably in the top 500,000 earners in the country, and was taking home up to ten times more than the average employed man who came to see him play on a Saturday afternoon at sixpence a time.

League cricket, however, was not just a means to earn large sums of money. Its one-day, all action format on a Saturday, from 2pm to 7pm, plus weekday evening matches in a knockout cup competition, was entirely suited to Constantine's adventurous disposition and all rounder status. He took to it like a duck to water. By contrast, he found English three day county cricket, with its carefully compiled totals, snobbish social divisions between amateurs and professionals, and its world weary players 'always looking around the horizon for a drop of rain', dull and uninspiring. 'One of the things that League cricket knocked into me was the knowledge that crowds will not pay to see robots play cricket,' he wrote later. 'It may be "cricket" under certain circumstances for two batsmen to camp at the wickets and knock up double centuries apiece in the course of two or three days, but the average cricket lover would much rather put down his money to see a sparkling 50 knocked up in half an hour.'

Although there was certainly a tradition of more enterprising cricket in the northern leagues, in reality Constantine may have done more to knock that ethos into league cricket than the other way around. For some years league clubs in Yorkshire and Lancashire had been employing overseas players as their single permitted professional among a team of top local amateurs: Constantine knew one of them, the West Indies cricketer Edwin St Hill, with whom he had opened the bowling at Shannon. But none before had such a galvanizing effect nor such a call on the public imagination as Constantine, and though many great Test players followed in Constantine's trailblazing footsteps, including George Headley and Garfield Sobers, none were ever able to reach the heights of popularity he attained in his nine years at Nelson – during which time the club won the League seven times and were runners up twice. James, among others, credited him with shaping 'the strategy, the style, the temper and the tone of league cricket' – not to mention the role of the professional – for many years to come. Quite simply, he was the best and the most popular league professional of all time. In the golden era of league cricket he was the golden player.

Constantine's first 1929 season for Nelson began in April, and it was a highly enjoyable one on the field. 'It opened out and enriched my life, because for the first time I was doing just what I enjoyed doing for my living,' he said. He played very well, taking 88 wickets in the season at an average of 12 runs apiece and scoring 820 runs at an average of 34. In subsequent seasons he performed even better, but he always maintained that the freedom

Fast and furious: though not tall, Constantine was a fearsome bowler in his prime, blessed with what Wisden called 'a bounding run, a high, smooth action and considerable pace'

and excitement of that first summer was the best of his life. Within weeks of arriving he had captured the hearts of the cricketing public not just in Nelson but across Lancashire – so much so that before long a local schoolmaster was reporting that a number of his pupils, posed the examination question 'who was Constantine the Great?', had written their answer as 'the professional at Nelson'. At the height of his powers and fitness, Constantine was able to give everything that was expected of him – and more. He added a new dimension to the role of professional and, in many ways, redefined it. While Constantine always wanted to win, it was his cricketing mission – unlike some professionals – to entertain. His acrobatic cricket brought him plenty of legendary figures: in 1933, in front of 8,000 people, he took all ten wickets against Accrington, clean bowling eight of his victims to finish the opposition's innings in just 39 minutes. In 1937, against East Lancashire, he hit the highest score of his career – 192 not out – while the next highest scorer could manage only 28. He hit 6,363 runs at 37.65 and took 776 wickets at 9.5 in his nine seasons at Nelson. In 1933, when he missed two of the side's matches to play Tests for the West Indies, he scored exactly 1,000 runs for Nelson at an average of 52.63 and took 96 wickets at 8.50. Once again, however, it was the nature of his performances that thrilled the crowds. The journalist and broadcaster Michael Parkinson, who saw him in the flesh as a boy, felt he played cricket 'like a man walking a tightrope without a safety net'.

The cricketing establishment may have paid little attention to the northern leagues, either then or since, but they were the most popular form of cricket in their day next to Test Matches, and Constantine appreciated that fact. Calder noted that 'a century solemnly grafted in five hours by a goodish county batsman off a mediocre attack in front of a few-score comatose spectators' would be recorded 'with some pomp' in *Wisden*, while a quick 30 struck by Constantine to win a vital League match 'cheered on by 10,000 highly excited people' would all but vanish from history. Constantine came to England already armed with a healthy scepticism about the supposedly elevated standards of the first class game, and his experiences in the Lancashire League confirmed him in that suspicion – even led him to argue, heretically and hugely ahead of his time, for the establishment of one day county matches and internationals. 'Many times I have been criticized, more in sorrow than in anger, for going into league cricket at all,' he said. 'I'll have read that I threw away my abilities and elected to join a game with technical inferiors in cricket skill. I only wish my critics had to face some of the batsmen and bowlers I met there, and to try to retrieve some of the situations with which I was faced. I resent the implication that I was taking things easy. To anyone who has watched a Lancashire League needle game, the innuendo is ludicrous enough. Never in my life have I played harder than in Lancashire.'

Constantine's unusually high regard for one day cricket and the talented amateurs who played it was one of the keys to his rounded success as a paid player in the leagues. Allied to his on the field pursuits, Constantine was the model professional off it. There was an early indication of his gracious and engaging style when, just a day or so after signing for Nelson – and still a greenhorn in terms of making public appearances – he was invited to give out the prizes before a large and curious audience at the Padiham and District Sunday School cricket league. 'He performed his task splendidly, and his speech of five or six minutes duration was a model of its kind,' reported the *Nelson Leader* newspaper approvingly. 'He spoke excellent English and was heard distinctly throughout a large cinema hall. Rev Wyatt of Burnley, the principal speaker, referred to Constantine not only as a cricketer but as a Christian gentleman, and in his reply Constantine said he followed his religion as much as he did his cricket. He could not say whether in his religion he had been successful, but if the voice of the people was the voice of God, then in cricket he had been successful. It was a thoughtful, modest little speech that made a direct appeal to the audience, who were sorry he did not speak much longer. He had a word for all the prize-winners, and in particular for a young boy who had won the prize for the neatest scorebook.'

Apart from his easy charm, Constantine, unlike some of his peers, was rarely if ever given to airs and graces or surliness when things didn't go his way. The Nelson club chairman Tom Morgan, at the end of Constantine's career, reported that he 'never gave the club a moment's trouble during the whole of his association with us'. To League cricket historian John Kay he was the 'perfect citizen of Nelson, an assiduous player coach (especially of children), and valued member of the local community' as well as being 'in every sense of the word a gentleman'. No sick supporter, said Kay, 'ever lacked a pre-match word or even a hospital visit [from Constantine] to provide the sort of medicine no doctor could better'. To the town's historian, Jeffrey Hill, he was its first 'true local champion'.

This was his fortunate lot as a club professional representing a small town rather than as a county professional with no such tangible attachments, and Constantine later acknowledged the beneficial effect that his public responsibilities, as well as his cricketing role, had on the development of his character. 'I am a better citizen for the time I have spent in Nelson,' he said. 'I am better materially, I am better socially. I have grown more tolerant, I have grown less selfish.' As much as anything, down to earth Nelson was a welcome release from the confines of Trinidad's race-bound society – and from the drudgery of the office work that Constantine had tried to make a go of. But being a professional in a foreign land had its own pressures. It was his job, very often, to bowl right through an innings and then to do most of the work in the batting department too. If he did not perform consistently – and entertainingly – then the likelihood was that his team would slip down the table and that crowds would dwindle, leading to financial pressures. Lancashire League standards at the time were at least as high as those on the county circuit, so it was no foregone conclusion that success would be his. Despite his touring experience, he was also relatively unfamiliar with the damp, grassy conditions of England, which posed their own problems. There were coaching duties and functions to attend – and he was essentially owned by the local community. Constantine could not walk out of his home without being recognized, and not just because he was just about the only black man in town.

In the early days at least, Constantine was often followed by a throng of curious small boys, most of whom had never seen a black person before. He was uncomfortable with this for a time, but was guided into acceptance by the more phlegmatic approach of his wife, who adopted a patient, slightly amused attitude to such trials.

For the first season Constantine and Norma left daughter Gloria behind with relatives – perhaps an indication that, despite the three-year contract, they wanted to leave their options open. They moved into a local landlady's two-roomed lodgings that had been arranged for them in Howard Street, near the town's Whitefield Elementary School in Nelson. Nelson was a typical gritty, close-knit Lancashire cotton mill town, just over the border from Yorkshire, and its inhabitants were not given to making a fuss about anything.

Although Constantine was almost immediately popular on the pitch at Nelsons' Seedhill ground, there was wariness on both sides in the town at large. Constantine didn't know what to expect, and neither did the people of Nelson. While the townsfolk had hosted other professionals before him, including the Australian Test bowler Ted McDonald in the early 1920s, they were unaccustomed to outsiders, and were doubly ill at ease with the sight of a black man in their midst. Constantine's curiosity value was high – children leaving the school opposite their home would often jump up at the front window so they could get a look at the strange new couple. There was always intense interest – and a fair amount of staring – when Norma or her husband ventured out to the corner shop for provisions. On one occasion, Constantine called at a local house where two little boys, aged four and six, were invited to shake his hand. 'The bigger boy was brave, almost blasé,' reported Constantine. 'His small hand gripped mine hard. The little one, however, seemed a trifle nervous, but he too gave me a good firm grip. Then as I turned again to speak to their father, I heard him whisper to his brother: "None's come off on me – look!", and he held out his hand palm up. "Has it come off on you?" he asked.' On another occasion, having befriended a little boy whose parents he knew, Constantine was met by the child in floods of tears after his first day at school. 'Uncle Learie, you never told me you were coloured,' he said. Constantine realized his classmates 'had given him a bad time when they discovered that he had a friend with a different coloured skin.' Typically, Constantine and the boy remained in contact as good friends throughout his life.

While there were welcoming letters from ordinary members of the public, there were abusive ones, often racist and usually unsigned. They generally told Constantine that he was not welcome and urged him to go home as soon as possible. He kept one or two of them in his papers until his dying days, including a letter dated 26 July 1933, postmarked Colne, which was addressed, politely enough, to 'L N Constantine Esq, professional, Nelson CC', but began 'Dear Nigger'. Mentioning recent newspaper reports about his hostile bowling, it warned him not to adopt such tactics in Saturday's forthcoming game against Colne. 'Well, Nigger, if you start bumping them on Saturday you will get bumped, not half, so try to play the game – and remember you are playing among white men and not niggers,' it said. Although there was plenty of general courtesy from the locals, there was little outward friendliness in the early days, and initially friendships were hard to come by. Constantine bore many of the jokes about his skin colour, and even told one or two against himself. But he was careful to set down boundaries too. When, in his first season, he ran out a team-mate on 49 and was called a 'black bugger' by the departing batsman for doing so, Constantine objected in no uncertain terms, and there were no further recorded incidents of that kind during his time there.

Later he put much of that early edginess down to ignorance and unfamiliarity rather than malice, and acknowledged that it took time to be welcomed into such a tight-knit community. But at the end of the first season he remained uncomfortable, and despite his success on the field had all but decided that he should break the three-year contract and return home for good. Norma, who in her largely housebound situation had borne even more of the early isolation, nonetheless persuaded her husband that they should stay and make a fight of it, reminding him of the frustrations and lack of progress back in Trinidad as well as the money and status he had newly acquired. 'My mother kept reminding him that he had come there to make it,' said daughter Gloria many years later. 'If he had gone there entirely on his own he probably would have never made it.' Constantine went with his wife's strong advice, as he nearly always did, and had already begun to feel better about the situation when he went on an end of season tour with Nelson to Scotland, a thoroughly enjoyable expedition during which the players asked him to be captain for the trip.

As if to emphasize Norma's point about the financial security that Nelson had opened up for them, the couple then spent some of the winter in New York as the guests of West Indian cricketers based in the city. The New Yorkers paid for the passage and accommodation of the famous Lancashire League cricketer and his wife in return for Constantine's appearance as top billing in a match involving the best local cricketers. When Constantine made one particularly good catch, the ecstatic spectators invaded the outfield, showering him with coins and dollar notes. 'There was nothing else to do but accept what the Gods provided, and a few minutes later I was bowling my fastest, with my pockets bulging, clinking like the fettered ghost in the ancestral hall,' he remembered. It was a reminder of the potential riches that could now come his way.

For the second season at Nelson, the couple came back from Trinidad with four-year-old Gloria, who was soon to attend Nelson Preparatory School. Her ice-breaking presence probably helped to soften attitudes and make the couple more at home – and in any case, the novelty value of having a black family in town was now less marked than it had been the year before. This time the Constantines

In good company: with the great English cricketer Jack Hobbs, who was a fervent Constantine admirer

lived in rented rooms in Buccleuch Street, just around the corner from their first digs. But by the end of the summer, flushed with savings, the family was able to rent a two-up, two-down, garden-less terraced house at 3 Lea Green Terrace, Meredith Street, in a more salubrious middle-class area in the higher part of town. For the first time, although Constantine toured Australia with the West Indies from November 1930 to March 1931, they lived in Nelson through the winter too, and the switch to Meredith Street helped them settle. Constantine later said that in Lancashire 'if they give friendship it is wholeheartedly given', and at last they began to enjoy themselves in local company. Nelson had never been hostile, but now it became distinctly friendly. The family began to go on day trips and picnics with groups of local people, and had some involvement with a local social club of mainly town hall workers – The Spuds – which would draw them into dinners and summer outings. Later on, when Constantine's brother Elias was playing as a batsman and medium paced bowler for Rochdale, the two of them, out on an excursion with other local families, repeated their childhood washing up trick of throwing the crockery to each other at a wayside café as the rest of the assembled party watched in horror and astonishment. Norma was never an outgoing type or a great joiner, but Constantine's raised status as club professional allowed them to make firm friends among a group of largely middle-class families in the area. They lived in Meredith Street for the next 20 years, until well after Constantine had stopped playing for the local team, and grew to love the place.

Though he was from halfway across the world, Constantine suited Nelson, for like the locals he was unpretentious, not given to bravura, nor overly concerned with status. His arrival at the club coincided with the beginning of the Depression, and as many of the cotton mills closed, he saw levels of poverty in Nelson that he had never witnessed so close at hand in Trinidad. Many of his fellow players were among the several thousand unemployed and the town was, for the most part, a poor one. Yet he was largely cocooned from any possible resentment by his performances on the field. For those – unemployed most of all – for whom his exploits on a Saturday afternoon at Seedfield were the highlight of the week, he did something for his money, gave them value for their sixpence and lifted the town's spirits. He also put Nelson on the map. Calder noted that local people even took pride in the fact that 'he was a 'perfect gentleman' who spoke 'beautiful English' in contrast to the Lancastrian accents of most. While he was one of the wealthiest people around, Constantine was always careful with his money, never given to ostentatious displays of wealth and would often hand over his match collections to local charities. He had an Austin Seven car – a rarity in those parts – but could often be found treating excited young children to rides around town, and he fitted in well with the non-conformist streak in Nelson by being a non-smoking non-drinker who didn't gamble. While he certainly had charisma, he had humility too. Club captain Harold Hargreaves, who had met him at Liverpool docks on the day he arrived to take up his post, called him 'a good man and a simple one'.

All of these qualities eventually allowed Constantine to find his place in Nelson. They also encouraged the locals to warm to him. But he was also helped by another factor: within a couple of years he had another Trinidadian with him in the town. CLR James, with whom he'd kept in sporadic contact over the past few years, had talked to Constantine about his idea of sailing to London and developing his writing. Constantine also had plans for a book about his early life and views on England, and in 1931 he broached the subject with James, suggesting he should come to England and help him to write it, living at his home in Nelson if necessary. Both men were excited by the project for, as James observed later in *Beyond a Boundary*, in those days cricketers who had not yet retired rarely wrote autobiographies, and very few West Indians wrote books at all. Although Constantine and James were hardly intimates, they knew enough of each other to suspect that they would get on reasonably well.

James took Constantine up on his offer. He set sail for England in March 1932, arriving in Plymouth as a gifted intellectual member of the black Trinidadian middle classes, having been an outstanding student who had won a scholarship to the island's premier school, Queen's Royal College. Born in the same year as Constantine, he had spent his subsequent years teaching at his alma mater, playing cricket for the brown-skinned middle-class club of Maple (even though he was as dark-skinned as Constantine), and dabbling in journalism as a reviewer and cricket writer in the local press. Incredibly well read, deeply anglocentric, and schooled in the classics, James shared with Constantine a passionate and thoughtful fascination with playing and dissecting cricket. But in many ways their common ground ended there. Although James was a good cricketer, his cerebral batting and bowling contrasted just as much with his contemporary's carefree abandon on the field of play as his effortless head-in-a-book progression through early life had contrasted with Constantine's laboured efforts as a clerk. While the pride and popular appeal of Shannon played a significant part in Constantine's politicization, James later conceded that he was 'stunted' in his outlook by choosing Maple, which 'delayed my political development for years'. During early adulthood James had shown little interest in politics or the struggles of ordinary black people, and felt that Constantine had a point of view that seemed 'unduly coloured by national and racial considerations'. Yet he found that his conversations with Constantine, particularly on Constantine's visits home after playing abroad, had gradually 'pecked at the shell' of his intellectualism. Once encouraged out of this shell, James advanced in leaps and bounds, moving quickly from a moderate left of centre viewpoint to strong support for communism and a celebrated career as a writer of political books such as *The Black Jacobins* and *State Capitalism and World Revolution*.

When he arrived in England, James initially spent a few weeks in London, hawking around manuscripts and ideas he had brought with him. But his money ran out in May 1932 and Constantine generously suggested that now was the time to come to stay up in Nelson. The move was to have a big impact on both men's lives. 'Up to that time I doubt if he and I had ever talked for more than five minutes on West Indian politics,' said James. 'Within five weeks we had unearthed the politician in each other. Within five months we were supplementing each other in a working partnership which had West Indies self-government as its goal.' The early thirties were a time of growing non-white agitation in the British West Indies as the minority white monopolization of power and economic influence, plus the effects of the worldwide Depression, drove many hundreds of thousands into stultifying poverty and angry dissatisfaction. The response was a burgeoning and fiery labour movement that brought forth the first significant stirrings of nationalism and a new striving for a black West Indian identity in areas such as the arts. James quickly grew to feel that together he and Constantine could help 'initiate the West Indian renaissance, not only in cricket but in politics, history and writing'. It was a bold claim typical of James's lofty aspirations, but one which they set about living up to in their various ways. They egged each other on.

Although Nelson was thousands of miles from the Caribbean, it proved a useful cradle for their activities. James found that the people of Lancashire had developed 'an inordinate appetite for asking Constantine to come to speak to them', most often at church or rotary club meetings – and that the very act of doing so had begun to crystallize many of their ideas. Constantine began taking James along to such meetings for company and moral support, and soon

James was either standing in for him or performing a double act, although 'neither he nor I had any illusions about the fact that I was travelling in his orbit'. Nearly always the topic of the meetings would be cricket and the West Indies. Audiences were keen to hear about life in Trinidad, and this inevitably led Constantine and James to talk of social and political conditions there. Constantine, said James, was 'a reassuring presence' on the platform who would talk passionately about race and nationalism yet would finish with 'a few pleasant and graceful words' that would unruffle any ruffled feathers. He was, after all, a professional cricketer, and wary of being too political in the public arena. James, by contrast, was freer from such constraints, tended to have a more confrontational edge to his contributions, and rapidly became as sought after at such engagements as his colleague. 'One evening as soon as I was finished, the chairman rose after applause and said: "Bless my soul if Mr James isn't as good at this business as Learie is at his,"' James recounted. 'The audience responded with a deep hum of approval. It is at such moments you know that old bonds have been cut away and new ones put in their place.'

Public meetings were not the only forum in which James and Constantine performed. Local people would regularly drop by Constantine's house for a chat, and kitchen table conversations often revolved around the politics of the local labour and co-operative movements. The town was occasionally known as 'Red Nelson' or 'Little Moscow', and a branch of the Independent Labour Party had been set up there before the turn of the century. The Labour dominated local council was an early hotbed of municipal socialism, with its emphasis on housing for working families and the provision of public facilities. Within a short time of being flung into such an arena, an energized James had joined both the Independent Labour Party and the League of Coloured Peoples, a body set up in 1931 to lobby for better treatment of black people in Britain. While Constantine discreetly signed up to the latter, he refrained from joining the former, conscious that he did not want to be seen to be taking up a consciously political role in the town. As a cricketer Constantine felt it was better to stay out of frontline politics, even at a local level, for he knew that if he strayed too far into that field it might compromise his relationship with the town. Partly, too, he was not yet ready for active politics, though he thought about it a lot. Off duty in his home, or in the throes of discussion in friends' houses, Constantine was a little freer with his ideas. He was broadly a man of the left, but much of his focus was distinctly West Indian and based around the politics of race. 'He had deep convictions. Not simply that he was as good as anybody else – in his own particular field he was better than most,' said James. 'His "they are no better then we" did not have a particular application. It was a slogan and a banner. It was ... the politics of nationalism.'

Unlike James, who had license to roam, Constantine had his cricket career to concentrate on. But he also realized that through the influence of the way he lived his life in Nelson – and his sporting achievements – he had a chance to make a point about racial equality that tied in neatly with his nationalist aspirations. His very presence in England created enormous interest in the West Indies and West Indians, and this could be turned to the advantage of his cause. For the time being, however, he had to operate on a lower political level, using his status in the community to quietly tackle ignorance. Although he valued James as an ally at this stage, Constantine also probably saw that his new lodger could act as his proxy, expressing views that he would be less willing to make known. James was free to explore avenues that were not really open to Constantine, and this he encouraged him to do. His new friend spent only a year in Nelson – 'a year of growth for both of us', said James – but Constantine did an inordinate amount for him, and effectively acted as his sponsor. As a consequence of the speaking engagements that Constantine put James's way, the new arrival was invited on to a BBC radio programme celebrating the abolition of slavery, and Constantine also helped James get regular work with the *Manchester Guardian* by encouraging him to send a cricketing article on Sydney Barnes to the great *Guardian* cricket writer Neville Cardus, whom Constantine knew. Cardus took James on, and that at least provided James with a regular income, relieving his host of some of the burden of supporting him.

Importantly, Constantine also helped to pay for the publication, in Nelson, of *The Case for West Indian Self Government*, a 32-page pamphlet written by James that contributed to the Caribbean nationalist struggles that began from that time onwards. James undertook to repay the money on sales, but it is not clear whether these ever covered the costs. More prosaically, Constantine and Norma provided a cosy, stable home base for James in his early days of political development. Once James had established himself in England with Constantine's help, he moved back to London, where the two kept in sporadic contact, though they drifted apart later. While there was early kinship with Constantine in Nelson, their relationship was not a lastingly intimate one. James was a handsome and charming womanizer whose often caddish extra-curricular activities and embrace of Trotskyism would eventually rub up uncomfortably against Constantine's strong moral views and dislike for dogma. Nevertheless, it is arguable that without that early mentorship and support, James may not have grown to make the contribution that he did to West Indian cultural life and politics. They remained lifelong acquaintances, even though they did not see eye to eye on all matters.

While Constantine had done a lot for James, James also did something for Constantine. His fellow countryman's diverting intellectual activities and late night debating sessions did not come without their drawbacks – and for a spell that summer Constantine had a terrible time with the bat, which James blamed on his distracting influence. Their relationship would constantly have been shaped by James's rather needy presence as a freeloading lodger. But James gave Constantine the confidence to move into the field of writing. More specifically, he wrote, with help from James, his first book, *Cricket and I*. Published in 1933 with a supportive foreword by Cardus, *Cricket and I* largely chronicled Constantine's cricketing development thus far, and aimed to explain some of the background to his life. It was, as James noted, 'the first book ever published in England by a world famous West Indian about people and events in West Indies'. It was also unusual, in those times, for a cricketer to write a serious autobiography while still playing. Henceforth, said James, 'the West Indies was speaking for itself in the modern world'. *Cricket and I* also brought into the open, tentatively and for the first time, some of the racial tensions that were undermining West Indies cricket. Specifically it talked of Constantine's frustrations at the imposition of a white captain on the West Indies side, and of the idea that the Test side could not make real progress until it was free from the deferential mindset that this engendered. While his comments may not seem to amount to much at this distance, some commentators have viewed the appearance of *Cricket and I* as a significant landmark in the struggle for West Indian self determination. The cricketing academic and University of West Indies professor Hilary Beckles, for instance, argues that its publication 'was a moment of conceptual rupture with colonialism' that inspired a number of other proto-nationalists to voice their own views.

James's presence in England also gave Constantine the impetus to start the educational studies that would set him out on the long road to becoming a barrister. For a while James himself began tutoring his friend in the Senior Cambridge Certificate, and although the lessons didn't last long, partly due to cricketing commitments, they at least planted a seed that was cultivated by Norma in later years. On a personal level, however, James was also a valuable West Indian companion in a town where it would have been easy to feel isolated. 'Apart from someone who went around collecting refuse in an old pushcart, Learie and I were the only coloured men in Nelson,' recalled James. 'That meant that wherever you went and whatever you did you were automatically under observation. Constantine lived the life placidly enough, but at times he would just pick himself up and on the slightest excuse go off to the anonymity of London, or even Manchester.' There were many acts of unspoken kindness from new friends – James noticed, for instance, that on cold days when Norma would privately be loathe to venture out, neighbours would casually stop by to see if she wanted anything from the shops. But Nelson's new citizens could never quite get rid of the feeling, as James said, that 'whatever we did would be judged as representative of the habits and standards of millions of people at home. You had to be mobilized so as to keep a steady head and not be betrayed into foolishness'. Nonetheless, James quickly grew to appreciate, as much as Constantine, the warm local glow that had wrapped itself around the household at Meredith Street. While the cricketer's charm, sense of fun, and easy manners had undoubtedly conquered Nelson, James saw that the Nelson people had also conquered him.

Constantine played for Nelson far longer than most professionals stayed at any club, but in the end, aged 38, he left the team he loved for Rochdale in the Central Lancashire League, for whom his brother Elias also now played. The money at Rochdale was slightly better than at Nelson: his surviving tax assessment forms for the year up to 5 April 1939 show his income as a professional cricketer was £812, mostly earned in just 20 weeks' cricket with his new team. But he knew he was now past his very best, wanted to begin to concentrate on studying for law, and in any case felt in need of a change. He was touched by the spontaneous response when the Nelson townsfolk heard of his departure – 'I could not walk half a mile through the streets without being stopped literally hundreds of times by all sorts of people … begging me to stay,' he said. But even the personal pleadings of the mayor had no effect.

He played a season for Rochdale in 1938, performing just as consistently but enjoying it less than he had hoped, and in 1939, with his international career drawing to a close, he chose to tour England with the West Indies rather than have another season in league cricket, even though he was out of pocket as a result. There were a number of things Constantine didn't like about the Central Lancashire League – he found it more mercenary, with players prepared, he alleged, to sacrifice their team's fortunes for the sake of scoring a slow 50 that would entitle them to a boundary edge collection; he found the slower pitches less to his liking, and he objected to jealous murmurings about his level of pay. More significantly, he became embroiled in a wounding dispute when he was racially abused on the field of play by an umpire who had controversially given him out. Word had reached Constantine's ears prior to the match – probably from his fellow Rochdale players – that derogatory remarks were being made behind his back by the opposition, and while he chose to ignore this, he erupted when the umpire voiced his own 'contemptible' remarks. Constantine asked Rochdale to take up the matter, and when they did so, he received a veiled threat of legal action from the Central Lancashire Umpires Association. Although Rochdale, in Constantine's estimation, proved themselves to be 'more indignant than I was myself' over the incident, an emergency committee of the League essentially brushed the issue under the carpet, conducting a closed inquiry that did not take evidence, according to Constantine, from any key witnesses to the incident, even though there were a number of individuals who were 'clamorous to make the whole thing public'. The committee judged that any remarks, if made, were part of a private but overheard conversation between the two umpires, and that this entitled them to say what they liked. The matter was closed. Constantine continued to live in Nelson until the late 1940s, and as its favourite son, was made a freeman of the borough in 1963. Wherever he went – and he continued to play in the leagues during and after the Second World War – he never quite found the same spirit elsewhere.

3 First-class citizen

League cricket at Nelson was the making of Constantine in many ways, but it also helped him to become a more successful top-level cricketer. Despite the impact he had made against the counties on the 1928 tour to England, his Test performances that season had been poor: he scored just 89 runs in six innings and took only five wickets at an average of 52. Constantine was not alone in under-performing in those three Tests, but his encounters with the touring MCC side of 1925–26 had barely been any better. There was a nagging doubt, for some at least, that he might not be able to produce results at the highest level.

Shannon had been a good proving ground in Trinidad over the years, and the annual inter-colonial tournaments for Trinidad against British Guiana and Barbados pitted him against some fine first class players. But before 1929 Constantine was not playing enough regular top level cricket for his own good. From the time he went to Nelson, however, things changed.

Apart from more or less regular twice-weekly appearances for his club, Constantine played 47 first class matches over the next two years – nine more than he had made in his career to date. He was now a full time cricketer, and it made a difference.

Significantly, the beginning of Constantine's impact on the international stage was his first post-Nelson Test match back home in the West Indies, in the winter of 1929-30, when he played against an England side that featured the likes of Patsy Hendren, George Gunn and Wilfred Rhodes. The first Test was notable for the arrival on the international scene of the great West Indian batsman George Headley with a century, but Constantine was declared the home star of that drawn match in Barbados for an all round performance that featured some spectacular catches close to the wicket and dogged bowling, including three for 121 off a draining 39 overs.

In the second Test in Port of Spain, which West Indies lost, he again bowled and fielded superbly, scored 52 in 50 minutes in the home side's first innings, and took six wickets in the match. But it was during the third Test in British Guiana that he made the most telling contribution, finishing with figures of four for 35 in England's first innings and five for 87 off 40 overs in their second – performances that helped bring West Indies their first ever win in a Test match. After the disappointing results of previous years and the constant struggle to establish themselves on the world stage, the significance of that result in the West Indies was hard to over-estimate. Constantine may not have won the game single-handed – far from it, as Headley made centuries in each innings and Clifford Roach made a double hundred – but he was the urgent, irresistible driving force behind the victory. The *Barbados Advocate* described him as 'a wonder', and by that third Test he had established himself not just as a popular player, as he had been for some time, but as an icon of West Indies cricket. Inter-

Favourite son: Constantine, with wife Norma, receives the freedom of Nelson years after they moved away; clearly the fondness of the Constantines for the town was reciprocated

island and racial politics meant that Constantine lost his place in the fourth and final Test of that series, in Kingston, to a Jamaican. But by then he needed to get back to England for his return to Nelson, and in any case he must have been relieved to have taken no part. The match was one of cricket's rare 'timeless Tests' with no scheduled end, and after nine days of combat – during which England ran up 849 in their first innings – the match was declared a draw so that the England team could catch the boat home. West Indies had drawn the series, and Constantine had been an instrumental figure on the Test stage for the first time.

After a second season at Nelson in the summer of 1930, Constantine returned to the Caribbean in the autumn to join the West Indies party as they sailed through the Panama Canal and across the Pacific on their first ever tour of Australia. There, between November 1930 and March 1931, Constantine met a formidable Australian team that included Don Bradman, the greatest batsman of them all. The tour was another personal triumph for Constantine, whose fast and fiery bowling, allied to his extraordinary fielding and hard-hitting batting, suited the Australian public's tastes down to the ground. He had felt a shade uneasy, in common with others in the side, about the sort of reception that black players might receive in Australia. But his worries were eased as soon as he stepped ashore. 'Throughout that tour there was never the slightest hint of any discrimination against us, either by onlookers or players or officials,' he said. 'We were treated as cricketers, given a magnificent time, and made to feel friendliness wherever we went.' He liked what he saw in Australia, and it got him thinking about how independence within the Commonwealth would benefit Trinidad and the other West Indian territories.

In fact the only racial tension he observed in Australia was within the West Indies team itself, mainly due to the appointment of the white Trinidadian and Cambridge Blue, Jackie Grant, to the captaincy. Constantine was exasperated by the fact that Grant, a stranger to most of the players, had come straight from Cambridge to skipper the West Indies without seeing any of his players in action. This led, he felt, to a lack of cohesion and direction in the team, something he believed would dog the West Indies as long as they had a white leader imposed from on high.

The West Indies did badly in the five Test series, losing 4–1. Nevertheless, they won their first ever Test abroad during the tour, at Sydney, where Constantine was deeply touched by the rare honour of having his photograph taken and placed in the pavilion. Despite the growing status of Headley, Constantine was again the popular hit of the tour, particularly in Sydney, where he had opened the visit with an explosive 59 in 35 minutes in the first match against New South Wales – described by the *Sydney Sun* as one of the most sensational innings ever played in Australia. In a second game against the same team before the final Test, after taking six wickets, he was run out for 93 in what he felt was his best ever first class innings. Unusually that knock did not contain a six, for he had been bet sixpence that he could not play an innings of more than 50 without lifting at least one shot clear over the boundary. Though not a gambler, Constantine was a great lover of dares, and he was delighted to break through another boundary, during that tour, by becoming the first batsman ever to hit the parsimonious aboriginal bowler E Gilbert for a six, in the match against Queensland.

He bowled tirelessly and with venom throughout the tour, and scored runs freely against the state sides. But it was the phenomenal agility and anticipation of his fielding that proved the biggest draw. In Sydney he was said to have taken a catch while executing a complete somersault, a feat which, if true, was astounding, and if not, then a good measure of the legend that attached itself to his game. Others later claimed to have seen him perform the same trick elsewhere, while Constantine said his habit of performing cartwheels while fielding had stemmed from younger, much poorer days when he dared not provoke his mother's ire by getting grass stains on his one pair of thin cricket flannels. Whatever the truth of the somersault stories, Bradman ranked him 'without hesitation' as the greatest fielder he had ever seen. Yet Constantine's performances with bat in the Tests were disappointing and his bowling only respectable at best. In all matches, he was the best of the frontline bowling on the tour with 47 wickets at 20.21 and took fourth place in the batting with 708 runs at 30.78. But in the Tests he scored only 72 runs in ten innings and took just eight wickets at an average of 50.87. One Australian commentator thought this was 'genius badly directed'.

The Australian tour was to be Constantine's only appearance against them. Test matches and tours were far less frequent in those days, and he would play just three more Test series – in 1933, 1934-5 and 1939. In fact, during the 1933 West Indies tour of England his Nelson commitments meant he was only sporadically available to play for the tourists, although he appeared at Lord's in May against the MCC, scoring a half century in 27 minutes and taking important wickets with hostile bowling to help West Indies to victory. Constantine was not released by Nelson for the first Test despite protracted negotiations between the West Indies board and his club. He would have liked to play, but did not see Nelson's stance as unreasonable given that he was being paid handsome money to turn out for crucial league games. After two excellent midweek performances for West Indies against Lancashire and Yorkshire, including nine for 94 in the match against the latter, he was given permission to play in the drawn second Test at Manchester, top scoring in the second innings with 64. Here, however, his performance was remembered more for controversy over allegedly 'dangerous' bowling by himself and his opening partner Manny Martindale. It was not the first time that Constantine had been criticized for aiming short pitched deliveries at Englishmen, but the 1933 tour was being staged in the wake of the most sensationally divisive of all cricket tours, England's visit to Australia in the winter of 1932-3, when the England captain Douglas Jardine had instructed his opening bowlers, Harold

Larwood and Bill Voce, to aim directly at the batsmen's bodies and heads with a strong leg side field. This 'bodyline' attack, and the injuries it led to had created so much ill-feeling among Australians that it severely strained relations between the two countries for a number of years.

Whether the West Indian bowling at Manchester was specifically bodyline was a matter for interpretation, but as Constantine later noted: 'bodyline was gunpowder in those days and the trained nose smelt it anywhere'. He was vaguely flattered that his efforts should be considered in the same vein, especially given that the pitch was easy paced and, now in his early thirties, he was some

In full flow: Constantine bowling for the West Indies at Chelmsford on the 1939 tour of England

way short of Larwood's pace. But for many England supporters it was the first chance they had been given to see something close to the intimidating tactic in operation – and they did not particularly like what they saw. While the damage was limited – Wally Hammond had to go off for a short while after being struck a painful blow by Constantine – the sight of two black fast bowlers giving England some of their own medicine was not a comfortable one. Hammond reflected ruefully that 'we started it, and we had it coming to us'. Within a year or so of the match, the rules of the game were changed to allow umpires to intervene when they thought bowling was dangerous.

Wisden, rather like Constantine, thought the bowling in that Test a 'somewhat pale imitation' of bodyline, but noted that 'what [Constantine and Martindale] did was sufficient to convince many people with open minds on the subject that it was a noxious form of attack not to be encouraged in any way'. While it would be wrong to attribute the subsequent rule changes in large part to the bowling of Constantine and Martindale at Old Trafford, the irony of the situation was not lost on Constantine or his team-mates. There were later echoes of the same situation in the 1980s, when the West Indies were often criticized for the kind of intimidatory fast bowling that had been viewed as fair game in the past for other countries.

In general, Constantine was dismissive of the fuss about bodyline; he felt that it was a legitimate tactic and objected only to the double standards that it had brought to the surface. His feeling was that if the English had used it against the Australians then he and other dark skinned bowlers should be able to use it too. He was also a great admirer of Jardine's 'untactful sincerity and vigour', a little of which he probably saw in himself – and was deeply impressed by the bravery that the England captain displayed in that Manchester Test as he stood up courageously to his own dastardly invention, scoring 127 in the process. The match was also supposed, in popular mythology, to have led to the invention of the term 'chinaman' as a name for a left-arm wrist spinner. If the story is to be believed – and there are other versions of how the term arose – Constantine's West Indies colleague Ellis 'Puss' Achong, just such a bowler and a Trinidadian of Chinese descent, had England's Walter Robins stumped. As Robins left the crease he blurted out: 'Fancy being out to a bloody Chinaman', to which Constantine allegedly replied: 'Do you mean the bowler or the ball?' After that, if the story is to be believed, the term stuck.

Given the controversy generated by the second Test at Old Trafford, it was perhaps as well that Constantine was unavailable to play in the third and final Test – which West Indies lost by an innings and 17 runs – due to his continuing duties with Nelson. Across the entire summer he played just five first class games for the tourists, scoring 181 runs and taking 14 wickets.

There were no other first class pickings for the next year or so, but in the autumn of 1934 Constantine made an eye-opening trip to India for some coaching and to play cricket of a high standard in the Maharajah's Gold Cup Tournament. To his delight, he visited the Taj Mahal and stayed in a gold encrusted maharajah's palace. To his despair he saw, behind the palace walls, the most desperate conditions among the masses. Rather like the poverty he had witnessed on coming to Nelson, the deprivation in India gave Constantine some pause to consider the racial references by which he had so often explained iniquity. His biographer, Gerald Howat, argued that although he was 'a fighter against social distinction between white and coloured peoples', he 'was less sure of his ground when faced with economic distinctions'. His trip to India also briefly threatened to upset the Indian racial order, when there was a campaign to recruit Constantine into the 'European' team that played annually in the Bombay Quadrangular competition against three other teams: the Hindus, the Parsis and the Muslims. Constantine was patently not European, but his supporters argued that if the European team was re-named the 'Christians' – as it should have been in any case to bring it into line with the religious themes of its opponents – then their West Indian hero would be eligible. Unfortunately, as Ramachandra Guha reports in his history of Indian cricket, *A Corner of a Foreign Field*, the 'white Brahmins' of the European team 'were afraid of losing their caste by enlisting non-Europeans' and the campaign came to nothing.

When Constantine arrived home to Nelson from India just before Christmas 1934, he received a cable asking him to play in the 1934-5 Test series against England in the Caribbean. Perhaps because his contribution to the 1933 series had been so limited, perhaps also because he had become inured to the disorganized state of West Indian cricketing administration and its insular politics, he does not appear to have expected the invite, and it appeared at his door too late for him to travel over for the first Test in Barbados, which West Indies lost. Nonetheless, he willingly accepted the offer, sailing over with Norma and Gloria to play the second Test in Port of Spain. He made his highest Test innings of 90 in the first innings but as West Indies strove for victory on the final day, Constantine was warned by the Australian umpire for intimidatory bowling and captain Jackie Grant, much to the bowler's disgust, took him off. The home crowd bayed relentlessly for the return of their local hero, and before long Constantine was back in the attack. It proved to be an epic finish that saw

Constantine, with only two balls of the match left, trap Maurice Leyland leg before wicket with a magnificent slower ball to win the match and prompt a euphoric pitch invasion. As ever, Constantine had been at the very centre of the action. 'Ten thousand people rushed the pitch,' he recalled later.

'We tried to dodge, but it was no good, and I found myself shoulder-high, swaying and bumping amidst yells and laughter. Why not be honest and say I enjoyed it like mad? It was one of the moments when one sipped nectar with the Gods.' Constantine again played well in the drawn third Test at Georgetown in British Guiana, and by the time of his arrival in Kingston, Jamaica for the fourth and final Test, he was being hailed by the Jamaican *Daily Gleaner* as 'the greatest and most attractive personality' West Indies cricket had ever had. 'His spectacular batting arouses joy and excitement in all crowds, his bowling is always productive of some rare feat … and his fielding, with its unbounded energy, long striding cat-like leaps, marvellous accuracy in effecting the most inconceivable catches and gathering of balls, just fascinates.'

That fourth Test in Kingston had special resonance for the West Indies, as, with the rubber standing at 1-1, victory offered the chance of a first ever Test series win. Typically Constantine was again in the absolute thick of things, not only taking six crucial wickets in a victory by an innings and 161 runs but, thanks to an on-field ankle injury to skipper Jackie Grant, who retired hurt, taking over the captaincy in the later stages of the game. Given the measures that the West Indies cricketing authorities had taken to ensure that no black man would ever captain a regional side, it was a great irony and huge source of delight to Constantine that he should be the man to lead the team at the moment of their greatest achievement so far. Not surprisingly it was one of his most cherished memories, and not least because it was the last competitive game he played in the Caribbean. There were no more Test series there before the Second World War, and Constantine had long been disqualified from playing for Trinidad in the inter-colonial tournaments due to an archaic rule that excluded anyone with professional status. He played just one more first class game in the West Indies when, on a visit to the Caribbean in January 1939, he was persuaded to turn out as a guest for Barbados in a friendly match against British Guiana in Bridgetown.

By then he was 38, and knowing that the 1939 West Indies tour of England would be his last, had decided to keep the 1939 season clear. He had deliberately signed only a one-year contract with Rochdale in 1938 to allow himself to play for the West Indies, and knew that to swap a league season for a touring one would leave him considerably less well off. After long talks with the West Indies Board of Control, he was paid £600 plus a small share of any tour profits, of which there turned out to be none. 'I was dissatisfied, and said so openly, as is my habit,' he recalled.

1939 was a rainy summer. West Indies lost the series, losing one and drawing two of the three Tests against a very strong England side featuring Len Hutton, Walter Hammond and Bill Edrich. While Constantine was still able to produce brilliant batting and remained an exceptional fielder, he had long since accepted that his fast bowling days were over. Coming off a shorter run and bowling at something like medium pace, he used all his knowledge and experience to deceive batsmen through changes of pace, flight and line. He had always been a great experimenter and was now wily in the extreme. What's more, he was still totally committed. Despite his age, *Wisden* had him down as 'the most unflagging member of a very alert side'. He bowled more overs (652.1) and took more wickets (103 at 17.77) than anyone in the side, and at an average bettered by only six Englishmen on the first class circuit that season. It was a satisfying end to what had occasionally been a spluttering international career, and he finished on a superb high note as, with war approaching and barrage balloons hanging over the Oval, he took five for 75 in England's first innings in the rain-affected third Test, including the scalp of Hammond. Then, coming in at 395 for six in West Indies' first innings, he let loose one last time, producing a thunderous 78 in an hour out of 103 scored while he was at the crease. *Wisden* said he surpassed even Bradman in his amazing strokeplay and was 'absolutely impudent in his aggressive treatment of bowling'. It was a fitting 'climax of audacious adventure' for an entertainer making his final bow on the international arena. In fact it was his last match of the summer, as the tour was cut short by the onset of war.

But for the hostilities, Constantine would probably have liked to continue for West Indies another season or two, but it was a timely juncture for him to stop. He generally enjoyed that last summer, and the public gave him a good send off. *Wisden*, too, honoured his passing by naming him as one of its cricketers of the year. He was, said the almanac, 'a cricketer who will never be forgotten, who took great heed that all nature's gifts should be, as it were, expanded by usage, a deep thinker and an athlete whose every movement was a joy to behold'.

There were, however, signs that his easy enjoyment of top level cricket was coming under strain in that final season. During the tour he was perturbed by what he saw as the increasingly negative outlook of West Indian cricket – anathema to a man whose whole career had been built on pyrotechnics. He did not always see eye to eye with those in the dressing room, and later complained that

'I was roundly condemned as old fashioned whenever I tried to put some gunpowder into the cricket'. One anonymous younger player, confirming as much while also alluding to some of the tensions that arose over Constantine's lengthy pay negotiations before the tour, told a journalist: 'I don't listen to Learie when he is talking cricket, but while he talks money I pay attention'. Now comfortably the oldest man in the side, Constantine 'had the impression that I was being slightly indecent, an old barnstormer among refined young actors'. He was also dog tired, and though he never refused to bowl, was often unhappy about the heavy workload he was given with the ball. Uncharacteristically, but pointedly, he went absent without leave from the team hotel one day so that he could get some relaxation in the countryside.

War, then, drew a comfortable veil over the end of Constantine's intermittent first class career. Compared with the many cricketers whose careers were cut short or ended entirely by the First and Second World Wars, Constantine was lucky: his best years had neatly spanned the gap between them. Yet he played only 119 first class matches in the 18 seasons up to 1939, which was not a prodigious return. How is one to judge someone who played so little frontline cricket?

The answer may be to refrain from judging him on that basis at all. Constantine's lack of first class experience was not unusual among West Indians of the inter-war years, who had only a few inter-colonial games and the odd Test tour to dabble with. The fact that he played so few first class games was no reflection on his ability, nor was it, in any particular way, relevant to an assessment of his greatness.

What would be more apposite is to examine how he actually fared in those 119 matches. The bare statistics show that in the

18 Test matches he played – in relatively weak West Indies sides against strong England and Australia teams – he took 58 wickets at an average of 30.10, which was respectable enough. In those same 18 Tests he scored 635 runs at an average of 19.24, which was nothing to write home about. In all first class games he took 439 wickets at an average of 20.48 runs apiece, which was very good, and scored 4,475 runs at an average of 24.05, which was moderate.

At Test level then, Constantine's returns were rather disappointing given his acknowledged talent – *Wisden* summed them up as 'poor'. In the small number of top level international matches he played, the most he could claim on the statistics was that he was a good Test bowler who was handy with the bat. On his first class record, however, he could certainly claim to be an excellent bowler who was also a decent batsman. Constantine accepted that his bowling was his main strength, while his batting, which could be devastating on occasion, was not consistently at the same level. He admitted in 1933 that 'I am by inclination … a bowler rather than a batsman'. But what he lacked in batting consistency he more than made up for in fielding excellence and he was probably the only player in the world who could win a Test place with his fielding alone. He took an excellent haul of 28 catches in 18 Tests and 133 in 119 first class fixtures, meaning he comfortably averaged more than one catch a game – which puts him on a par with the best slip catchers in history. The vast majority of those top catchers, however, have been batsmen who have benefited from the luxury of standing at slip at both ends while their team is in the field; Constantine was invariably bowling at one end. When you factor in this exceptional fielding, then he has a watertight claim to being a genuine and very good all rounder at both Test and first class level. Certainly he was the best West Indian all rounder of his generation, probably the best all rounder in the world.

But a cricketer's greatness does not lie in the figures alone. What the bare statistical bones don't reflect is the sheer impact that Constantine had on the cricketing stage; his charisma, his exuberance, the capacity for being in the right place at the right time. 'It is really wonderful what an effect Constantine has upon any side with which he is playing,' said the Trinidadian batsman Andre Cipriani in 1932. 'His vitality seems to be contagious and his very presence is bound to be an asset.' Britain's first sports minister, Denis Howell, once told how, as a young man, he was so exhilarated by watching Constantine in the flesh at Edgbaston that he had experienced a 'spiritual uplifting'. Noel Wild, long-time friend, sports writer and editor of the *Nelson Leader*, noted that whatever the arguments about the individual components of Constantine's game, there was 'certainly never a more electrifying cricketer' in the game. 'He had an effervescence both on the field and off it that was both thrilling and infectious,' he said. 'You could just not be miserable when he was on the cricket field, and you just cannot be miserable when you are in his company.' Neither Howell nor Wild were alone in such feelings. Whether taking a crucial wicket, turning a game with some exhilarating batting or lifting a side with a breathtaking catch, Constantine possessed a rare capacity for the extraordinary that was recognized throughout the sport. 'His batting could win a match in an hour; his bowling in a couple of overs, his catching in a few scattered moments,' said *Wisden*. 'This was the kind of cricket nearest his heart: and he expressed himself through it. No man ever played cricket for a living – as Constantine needed to do more desperately than most professional cricketers – with greater gusto.' *The Times*, after his heroics during the 1928 tour, declared Constantine 'the most determined match winning cricketer in the world'. A little of that eccentric and intimidatory zeal was recalled affectionately in 1937 by the old England cricketer Fred Root, who had appeared against Nelson for Todmorden in a Lancashire League match. Tommy Carrick, the Todmorden wicketkeeper, known far and wide for his constant appealing, was behind the stumps when Constantine was batting, and as a Root ball hit Constantine's pads, Carrick, true to form, shouted a loud 'How's that?' for leg before wicket. 'Connie, with all the agility which only he possesses, leapt around like greased lightning, leered at Carrick and howled "Not out!". The little wicketkeeper was really scared. When he got to my end, he said: "Freddie, he's feared me; I don't fancy appealing any more. I thought he was going to bite me." "He won't hurt you," I replied. "It's only his excessive keenness." Two or three balls later, Carrick appealed again, and Connie went through the same performance. My words had made Carrick bolder. Assuming an air of outraged dignity and pointing to the umpire, he faced the West Indian like a pugilist and said to him: "Thee shurrup. I'm not asking thee, I'm asking t'umpire!"'

Apart from his great will to win and his superb technical attributes, Constantine was also, as Manley acknowledged, 'one of the greatest personalities the game has ever known'. Howat noted that no statistic 'stood comparison with the spirit of adventure and the sheer pleasure of playing which encompassed all he did on the cricket field'. That is where his true greatness lay. It would be stretching it to say that he was a great Test cricketer – or even that he was one of the great first class cricketers. But he was undoubtedly one of the greats of the game. More specifically he was a great of the West Indian game, and a towering presence in league cricket.

In both arenas he was an icon whose achievements and influence on the way the game was played far outshone any dry analysis of averages and aggregates.

For West Indies, Constantine's significance lay in his inextricable involvement with the main landmarks of early West Indies cricket: he took the first wicket for West Indies in Test cricket, was a key figure in their first Test win, played a handy part in the first Test win abroad, was captain and wicket taker when they won their first series. He was a catalyst who played a major role in earning the West Indies the respect they so craved in those early years. Manley credits him and Headley with launching the 'first great era' of West Indies cricket from 1928-39, 'opening the door of international cricket' – and therefore building the platform for the feats that were to come much later. For the rest of the world Constantine was the first West Indian to receive widespread recognition from the cricketing public and – more specifically – recognized by his peers and the public at large as the greatest black cricketer of his day, even when the dominant George Headley emerged before the Second World War.

Some, including Calder, have argued that this popularity stemmed from the fact that Constantine's extrovert, exciting qualities 'both disarmed and appealed to the racism of the period' which was happiest accepting the black man in the role of entertainer. While there may have been some truth in this, it does nothing to diminish the fact that, as Neville Cardus said, Constantine was a 'representative man' who was deeply conscious of what he stood for on the cricket field. Many people, both black and white, appreciated that. Cardus, in fact, argued that Constantine's cricket was 'racial' – meaning that he personified the attributes and mindset of the black West Indian cricketer. While that idea might these days come under attack for being politically incorrect and too much of a generalization – and Manley noted that 'Constantine's extrovert exuberance was, of course, more particularly Trinidadian than generally West Indian', it at least conveys the idea that Constantine was a black West Indian to the core, and that he meant this to show through in his cricket. It was a quality that Sir Vivian Richards possessed many years later, and it was an attribute of which Constantine was acutely aware and proud – so much so that he went as far as presenting himself as a preserver of the 'essential character of West Indian Cricket'. James felt that just as the great Indian-born cricketer Ranjitsinjhi made the British public aware of India in the late 1800s, so Constantine's cricket 'made them aware of the Caribbean in general and of black men in particular'. The nature of his game came to define what has remained to this day as the popular conception of the way West Indian cricket is, and should be, played – as Manley put it: 'that aggressiveness that is somehow good natured and which is the distinctively West Indian quality in all sport'. Constantine was, as the Barbadian cricket academic Hilary Beckles says, 'the first truly great West Indian superstar', a man who 'symbolised the spirit of West Indian fast bowling and athletic fielding' and established an 'ideological tradition' later followed by the likes of Headley, Worrell and Richards. Cardus felt he was as iconic to the West Indies game as WG Grace had been in England, while Clayton Goodwin, in his book *Caribbean Cricketers*, declared that Constantine 'personified the spirit of Caribbean cricket'.

In much the same way, he also managed to define and personify the spirit of league cricket. In the Lancashire League he really can be considered as a great on the statistics alone: with Nelson and Rochdale from 1929-37, he scored 6,673 runs at an average of 38.35

and took 790 wickets at 9.9. Even accounting for the supposed lower standards at that level – something that Constantine did not buy into – he was a dominant and consistent performer whose presence was the key to Nelson's triumphs. But again his claim to greatness in the leagues lay more in the way he played the game than in the bare statistics. He established the idea, more than any paid player before him, that the professional's role was not just to score runs and take wickets but to entertain. He became the forerunner of the modern one day cricketer. And crucially he also drew new levels of respect for league cricket in much the same way as he helped to gain coinage for the West Indies side. John Kay argued that Constantine 'earned for league cricket a new image as well as world-wide publicity', while Constantine's journalist friend Denzil Batchelor called him simply 'the incarnation of revolutionary cricket'.

James, among others, characterized Constantine as a league cricketer who played Test cricket, and not the other way round. Certainly his achievements in the leagues brought him as much, if not more, satisfaction than anything he did at first class level and for this reason, as well as the financial rewards, he was never worried that he did not play more in the first class game. Unusually for anyone before or since, he felt that the one day game was the purest form of the sport, and that even Test cricket, in the words of the inter-war South African fast bowler Sandy Bell, was 'not a game at all – just a battle from beginning to end'. The fact that Constantine did not play more at the 'highest' level often appeared to worry his critics and fans more than it ever concerned him. Instead, Constantine was conscious that his contribution to cricket lay in the nature and impact of his play as much as in the specifics of what he did or where he played. He showed only cursory interest in batting and bowling figures, would never play more circumspectly, for instance, when he was approaching a century, and complained that an obsession with averages had become the bane of cricket in England by the time he had retired from the first class game. Uncle Victor Pascall had once told him he could become the greatest batsman in the world if he practised hard enough, but Constantine was not interested in such goals. 'What I liked was to hit the ball hard, to hit it often and to vary my strokes,' he said. He lived by the sword and died by the sword: if his audacious hitting came off, then he was praised to the skies; if he was out early then he was often criticized for a lack of application. Maybe Constantine would have been able to get his head down and improve his batting average over time, but that was not the way he wanted to play. In his formative teenage years, when he proudly told his father that he had stuck around to score 19 in an hour for Victoria's second eleven, he was castigated for wasting his time at the crease. Thenceforth he would play for enjoyment, an outlook that earned him, even in those far off days, a reputation for being an 'old fashioned' cricketer. He revelled in the unorthodox, playing shots through his legs and, on one famous occasion against the MCC at Lord's in 1933, deliberately lifting a ball directly over the wicketkeeper's head for six. He once said that hitting a huge six at Lord's 'satisfied my soul as few things in life have done', and he was indeed the biggest of big six hitters. He is one of only three players officially recognized as having hit a six over the enormous (and now deceased) lime tree inside the boundary at Kent's headquarters in Canterbury – becoming the first batsman ever to do so when playing for the West Indies there in 1928.

Constantine, then, was an indisputably great cricketer, though you would not necessarily know it from the figures. He continues to find his way into many experts' all-time XIs. His greatness lay in the sheer vivacity and aggression of his play and in his ability to shape events. He was never a man to muddle his way through a game, even in injury, and was always intent on making some kind of impact. Very often, of course, he made no impact, but that was more likely to be because he had taken risks that had not come off rather than the fact that he had not played well. In that sense, at least outside of league cricket, he was consistently inconsistent, particularly with the bat. But there is little evidence that he ever went through a long patch of bad form. At the end of the 1939 season, as he looked forward with foreboding to the beginning of war, he looked back with pride on a cricketing career that had lit up the inter-war period.

4 War and welfare

The war was a turning point for Constantine. It ended his frontline cricketing career when he might have been tempted to strive for a few more years at the crease; it set him on a new course in public service; it finally freed him to tackle issues of race that he had long held back upon, and it underlined to him that he was now a citizen of Britain rather than of Trinidad. When the 1939 West Indies tour was cut short in late August, he could easily have journeyed by boat from Greenock with the rest of the players to the Caribbean. But he had not lived in Trinidad for a decade, and his family roots were now in Lancashire. Besides, he felt he owed something to the country that had adopted him. 'I would have felt like a rat deserting a sinking ship,' he said.

The onset of war gave Constantine little time to ponder on the new directions he was taking. He became involved in phoney war preparations – such as the sandbagging of Nelson's Reedyford Memorial Hospital – and volunteered as an air raid equipment officer with Nelson Borough Council (although it turned out that Nelson was never bombed during the war). Keen somehow to resurrect his aborted career in the law, he had accepted an offer from a fellow Nelson cricketer, Alec Birtwell, to work in his family solicitors' firm. But as work dried up with war approaching, he took up a post as a billeting officer with Nelson corporation, inspecting and grading local houses in readiness for evacuated children from Bradford and Manchester. This was an eye opener for Constantine, who, despite being aware of the poverty in Nelson, had rarely seen at first hand the daily living conditions of the poorest people in the town. 'I never knew until then the extent of the slums and poverty,' he said in a broadcast later. 'It would do many of my countrymen good to see and appreciate this for themselves.'

Despite his age, Constantine could still theoretically have been called up for military service. In fact he was preparing for a pre call-up medical examination in Blackburn when he received word from the Ministry of Labour and National Service in 1941 that he was wanted instead on civvy street. The job on offer, which he had applied for, was the fairly senior but temporary civil service post of Welfare Officer, which would require him to look after the interests of hundreds of West Indian technicians and trainees in the northwest who had been drafted in as factory workers to help the war effort. Around 20,000 black people lived in the docklands of London, Liverpool, and Cardiff during the war – many of them hastily recruited from rural areas of the Caribbean into manufacturing jobs, often in munitions factories, for which they had no skills. The government needed someone to act as their advocate, and Constantine accepted the task.

Supported by an assistant, Sam Morris (who was active in the League of Coloured Peoples) and a small group of clerical staff, he began work in October 1941. He was based initially in the Royal Liver Building in Liverpool, either commuting to the office by train or car two or three times a week, or often living the whole week and sometimes weekends in a Merseyside hostel, spending much of his time on factory and home visits. It was in Liverpool that he experienced wartime bombing close at hand. His office was responsible for helping the mostly young West Indian factory workers to find accommodation, get training, deal with any difficulties they had in their work, settle disputes, help send remittances back home, and generally ease their adaptation to a puzzlingly hostile local environment. Most were ill equipped for life in the grey industrial north of wartime England, and at times their demands frustrated Constantine, who, as a hardened settler, found the naivety and niggles of the young immigrants rather taxing. 'We had to do everything for them – as you would for children,' he once complained. He was though, on the whole, deeply sympathetic to the plight of those he was asked to be an advocate for. They suffered many of the indignities that he had already experienced, yet without the buffer of his unusual status and financial comfort. Even though his charges were in England to help the war effort, they often faced suspicion, hostility and downright racism. They were discriminated against in all manner of ways, not least in the quality of their housing, their wages and their working conditions. While some of the difficulties they encountered were down to straight culture clashes, they often found that employers would just not take on black people, while others tried to impose various forms of segregation.

Constantine's job was to act as a buffer zone between the races, promoting understanding where he could and working to ease relations through a combination of persuasion, guile and enforcement. This he did by working skillfully and closely with the trade unions, though they were not always willing allies.

Recognizing the suspicions and hostility of the white workers, who often harboured resentment that unskilled foreigners might be settling to permanently take the jobs of local people, he secured temporary union membership for the new recruits, thus not only emphasizing the temporary nature of their presence, but going some way to showing they were not just outsiders. Union membership also brought the West Indian workers more securely into the fold when it came to pay and work conditions.

Showing the kind of thoughtful improvisation he was known for on the cricket field, Constantine also brought his aptitude for lateral thinking to the fore. When he found that some employers were stubbornly refusing to employ West Indians, he used the ministry to press their companies for urgent deliveries of orders, forcing them to take on whoever they could get – black or white. Although prepared to be outspoken, his preference was for talk rather than outright confrontation, and he was particularly successful in dealing with a strike of African merchant seamen, of whom there were also many based in Liverpool during the war.

But while he preferred gentle dialogue, Constantine was quite prepared to stand up to officialdom. He later recounted the case of a West Indian seaman who came to his office because the captain of the Greek ship he had been working on had docked (or 'logged') all his wages on spurious disciplinary grounds. He was then thrown off the ship, penniless, with a warning that the police would be called if he caused trouble. 'I wrote for an appointment with the Greek consular official in Liverpool to discuss the matter,' said Constantine. 'I arrived at the time requested, was kept waiting half an hour, and was then rudely told to go, and call again two days later. I did so. I was then told: "The captain was in the right." Seeing that I was expected to go, I said mildly: "It is illegal to take the whole of a seaman's wages because he is logged." The reply was: "Your man is a liar. He had his wages." I am used to judging men, and after careful examination I was quite sure this man was not a liar. I said: "I prefer to take his word." That maddened the consular official. He rose slowly to his 6ft 3in height, glared at me, and snapped out in Hitler-like tones: "You may go! The interview is ended!" I responded: "The interview is ended. I shall expect the cheque for the wages tomorrow morning." A cheque for over £100 arrived next day.'

While he had already had his own experiences of racial discrimination in the decade since he had moved to England, the Welfare Officer job gave Constantine many more incidents to add to his collection. On one occasion he was asked to intervene in a dispute at a powder factory that employed thousands of people. Some white residents of a hostel erected to house workers there had objected to having to live with black workers under the same roof. Constantine took a private room in one of the hostels and went to live there for a time, in the hope that 'the white workers could see that I was an ordinary sort of person like themselves, and then might be willing to try some other coloured people as acquaintances'. Although the idea 'proved quite successful', while living there he ran into trouble one night when he decided to go out for an evening at the hostel's dance hall. As he was standing at the far end of the hall, talking to a group of male and female friends, an American Air Force officer 'aggressively shouldered the whole length of the hall' and shouted: "Get out, we don't allow nigs to mix with white people where we are". When Constantine politely but firmly told the man to 'go away,' the American replied: 'Get out nigger, before I smash you.'

'I said to the American, "Come outside with me," and I had every intention of thrashing him,' said Constantine later. 'I could have done it. I had marked the spot where I should hit him a formidable blow. But walking the length of that hall cooled me – I became aware of the newspaper headlines that would have resulted, and the general inflammation of the black and white problem that it would have caused, with England at that time filled with black and white American troops. So, rather sadly, I handed him over to the porter at the door and he was promptly ordered outside.'

Constantine's reaction that night neatly encapsulated his lifelong response, as a public figure, to racism: initial boiling anger coupled with a forceful attempt to nip the problem in the bud, followed by a more diplomatic approach influenced by the long term negative ramifications of how he might have dealt with the problem. He always preferred a mannered response rather than an off-the-cuff aggressive reaction, reasoning that it worked better to portray the aggressor as undignified and unreasoning – to show that it was the perpetrator who was the sad victim of racism, not himself. On many occasions he managed in this way to make his opponent look the fool while he cast himself as the winner. There was perhaps also an element of self-preservation about this subdued approach, for Constantine often said he could multiply the stories of personal slights indefinitely. 'I have learned to take them as an unpleasant part of daily life in Britain for anyone of my colour,' he said. 'They hurt, of course, but one tries to be philosophical afterwards. Long ago, an old Negro told me: "Learie, the only thing to do to with people with bad manners is to forgive them; any other way hurts more." He was right.'

While this stance later caused him some problems with more radical black figures who believed he was too soft by half, it served Constantine well and, in the long run, may have had a more concerted effect than mere confrontation.

His measured approach also meant he was well equipped for walking the tightrope that was the Welfare Officer job. Quite apart from the fact that he was West Indian himself, with first hand knowledge not just of the customs and psyche of West Indians but many years experience of the foibles and difficulties of life for a black man in England, he was well suited to the diplomatic demands of the post. The fiery Bessie Braddock, Labour MP for Liverpool Exchange while Constantine was in post, said he had shown 'all the tact in the world, and common sense as well' while carrying out his duties. It certainly helped that he was a famous cricketer, for Constantine had raised status both among the black workers and the host community – and he could always talk cricket to break the ice or leaven the negotiations. When some West Indian workers went on a wildcat strike in one factory to complain about discrimination, he used his persuasive powers to address the issue at hand and entice the workers to go back to work – only to find that the white workers then wanted their black colleagues to be fined for taking illegal industrial action. In the end he smoothed over the ruffled feathers by distracting the angry white workers with 'some cricket gossip' and the grumbles were forgotten. Sometimes he had to show just as much tact to address difficulties caused by those he acted on behalf – as in 1943, when mourners at the funeral of a Leeward Islands worker hired seven limousines to ferry them in style to the wake and then disappeared without paying. He organized for funds to be paid to the undertaker so that the bill could be settled.

Often Constantine could also use his personal charm to gain an audience from both sides. But his easy relations with the local people did not always work to his advantage, for some black workers felt his familiarity with white managers showed he was not on their side. Nor did it help that he was so obviously a black man apart – well dressed, comfortably off and, after years in the country, acclimatized to many of the local customs. His ministry colleague Sam Morris said that while most 'paid him the greatest respect as an understanding elder brother figure, some were skeptical … of his genuineness and dubbed him a black Englishman'. He worked within those confines, however, in a most successful way. As in his cricket, he had a strong work ethic, and was by all accounts a popular, jovial boss who generated a happy but hard working atmosphere in the office. When he finished shortly after the war, his workmates presented him with an illuminated scroll by way of thanks, and it was one of his most prized possessions. While the job was often an onerous one that tested his reserves of patience and diplomacy, it gave him great satisfaction and showcased his talents to a wide range of people, not least the Minister of Labour Ernest Bevin, with whom Constantine became friendly. Moreover, it was the kind of relatively elevated civil service job that would not have presented itself to him in race-conscious Trinidad, or for that matter, perhaps, in pre-war peacetime England.

It also brought him into closer contact with the League of Coloured Peoples, of which he had been an inactive member before the war. Constantine's private papers show that on a number of occasions he personally referred cases to the League when he felt frustrated by his own ministry's lack of progress or found himself unable to apply more pressure for a solution. In particular he passed on several cases of discrimination experienced by West Indians in the social sphere, including, in August 1944, that of a Jamaican merchant navy man, LeRoy Hammond, who was refused entrance to the Plaza Dance Hall in Glasgow on grounds of his colour. Often such cases would come to Constantine through personal correspondence, or as a result of his local renown, rather than directly through his job.

Constantine also drew the League's attention to a raft of difficult local cases in which white women had given birth to children after liaisons with black West Indian or black American servicemen stationed in the UK. Very often this resulted in mother and child being ostracized or the infant being abandoned. As a result of dealing with such cases, Constantine became a leading light in a project, supported by the League of Coloured Peoples and Pastor Daniel Ekarta of the African Churches Mission, to create a children's home for mixed race boys and girls who had been abandoned by their parents. The home was initially to have been named after the black American activist, Booker T Washington, and appears to have been granted permission to operate in July 1945. But the plans never reached fruition. Constantine reported several years later that a suitable property had been earmarked for purchase in Leeds, but that restrictions on the use of the building had scuppered the sale. There was then local opposition to such a home 'when we looked elsewhere'. Most of the money raised for the venture, including hundreds of pounds from Constantine-organized charity cricket matches, was eventually given to other good causes, including the Royal Infirmary in Liverpool. Although the matter appears to have been wound up in good order, the experience left Constantine angry and rather disillusioned. 'I was unhappy at this further experience of furtive opposition to any effort to help these coloured children,' he said.

Constantine's involvement with the League of Coloured Peoples peaked in and around the war years, when the League itself was at the height of its influence. Founded by Harold Moody, a Jamaican-born GP who had moved to London in 1904 to study medicine, the

League organized a three-day conference in July 1944 to draw up a 'Charter for Coloured People' that in some ways pre-empted the resolutions of the fifth Pan-African Conference held in Manchester the following year. The charter called for full self-government for colonial peoples at the earliest possible opportunity, and insisted that 'the same economic, educational, legal and political rights shall be enjoyed by all persons, male and female, whatever their colour'. It also demanded that 'all discrimination in employment, in places of public entertainment and refreshment, or in other public places, shall be illegal and shall be punished'.

Constantine was in regular contact with Moody, who was, in many ways, a man after his own heart. Historian Peter Fryer's description of Moody as 'precise and lucid in his writings and speeches, passionate in his emotions but controlled in their expression, tireless in his devotion to his life's work', could just as easily have been written about Constantine. Both influenced each other with their essentially moderate brand of racial politics, and the League held its 12th annual meeting in Liverpool in March 1943 – the first time it had done so outside London – largely because of its links with Constantine.

During the war Constantine also agreed to join the Liverpool Committee for the Welfare of Coloured Folk, though with little enthusiasm, as it was a largely white body led by the Church of England. He had come into contact with the Anglican Bishop of Liverpool, Albert David, during his war work, and their relationship was courteous but strained, as the Bishop himself noted. After David's death in 1944, Constantine said publicly that he found the Bishop 'inflexible' on matters of race, observing that while he espoused concern for black people in Britain, 'all he appeared to want ... was to keep the coloured people sufficiently fed and clothed and housed … but definitely in their place'. It was not the first time Constantine had come up against the Church's double standards on race. Although born and educated as a Catholic, he had lost most of his respect for organized religion in adult life, and though he still considered himself a Christian, was deeply upset, in particular, by the Catholic church's attitude to race. He had encountered, both personally and through slights to friends and family, numerous examples of prejudice in the church, not least when as a young man in Trinidad a black friend had been relieved of his cherished position as an acolyte in his local church after white members of the congregation had complained to the priest at the sight of a black man serving at the altar. The moment that finally confirmed Constantine's breach with the church, however, took place on his cricketing trip to New York in 1929, when, kneeling for a quiet moment of prayer towards the front of a church in the city, he was roughly interrupted by a white verger who told him: 'Git out o' there! Niggers at the back!'

'I have had some of the most painful experiences of colour segregation that I have ever suffered in churches in America, the West Indies and England,' he said later. 'Somehow if such things happen in cricket or in business, one is to some extent armoured against them, but when kneeling and praying, one's armour is off and the hurt seems to enter one's soul.' He went on: 'I have ceased to practise my religion. I do not make confession or attend mass any more and if I felt I were dying, I do not think I should send for a priest to give me absolution. I would take my chance of God's forgiveness. This is a dreadful thing for a sincere Roman Catholic to say, but I say it because I have suffered so much, and seen my coloured friends suffer so much, at the hands of white priests and white Roman Catholic worshippers.'

Although he was never remotely tempted to become a Muslim, Constantine approved of the way that Islam had 'broken down all barriers of colour and caste', and regretted that the Christian churches could not do the same. Nonetheless he still believed in the 'true Christian spirit' of loving one's brother and took this into his racial politics, trying always to show forgiveness. And he felt that a growing irreligiousness was in some ways responsible for race problems – that 'in exactly the same proportion as Christianity dies out of hearts of all colours, so hatred grows'.

With the war over, personal papers show that by October 1945, hinting at mild disillusionment with his job as well as a keenness to shape a new post-war life in other fields, Constantine had offered to hand in one month's notice to his employers 'unless the department has very good reasons for asking me to hold on'. He also sent a long letter to his regional controller complaining of a lack of action to help repatriate at least 30 unemployed West Indian technicians who had made it clear for some time that they were ready to return to the Caribbean. Nothing had been done despite his urgings on the matter, and as a result 'a large number of men are, in the most questionable quarter of the south end of Liverpool, forced by ... wicked fate to spend much of their spare time and find recreation in that unlikely circle'.

The ministry politely refused Constantine's offer to go, so he continued in post until the summer of 1946 while his unit was being broken up, tying up loose post-war ends that mainly involved helping the smooth return of West Indians to their homeland on passages paid for by the British government. Such arrangements did not always go to plan, and Constantine was sometimes required to intervene – as he did when 40 West Indians sailing home from Southampton were told they had to scrub the decks to pay for their passage home, even though their tickets had been paid for by the authorities. When there was an uprising on board, Constantine rushed down to speak to the various parties, and was able to give assurances to the men that they would in fact only have to do a minimal amount of tidying up and plate washing 'such as all passengers did in those days on converted troopships'. This was indeed the case throughout the journey, although Constantine later discovered that while the black passengers had tickets entitling them to proper bunks like everyone else, they were made to sleep in hammocks. This angered him, not least because he felt the men might feel he had duped them into sailing on false pretences.

Shortly after his eventual departure from his Welfare Officer job, on 2 May 1947, Constantine was made a Member of the British Empire (MBE) in recognition of his service with the ministry. He had made a success of his mission, and while his appointment had been good news for those West Indians who had seen their wages, accommodation and general welfare improve as a result of his interventions, it had also been good news for Constantine himself. For the first time in England he had been given the chance to actively engage himself on race equality issues that had mattered to him considerably over the previous years but which, given his apolitical existence as a cricketer, he had felt restrained from addressing. In many ways he suffered in silence during his cricketing years; now the Welfare Officer job, with its wide brief to roam around the thorny matter of race relations, was something of a release. It allowed him, within the confines of a certain neutrality expected of the job, to put himself firmly into the zone of racial politics. But with its emphasis on constructive dialogue it also fitted neatly with Constantine's idea that talk was usually the answer. On a more careerist level, it was a fairly high profile, though not especially high ranking, appointment that drew his worth to the attention of a number of people in power.

Other avenues opened up to Constantine as a result of his job, for the government had also used him during the war in a wider role to lecture services personnel about the West Indies and to encourage greater understanding of the culture of those black servicemen they were now fighting with. During the latter part of the war, still in his capacity as Welfare Officer but also in an echo of his early Nelson years, he spent many days and evenings giving talks to schools, clubs and various other organizations, including the Co-operative Holidays Association, the Reform Club in Manchester, the Young People's Guild in Wigan, and the Southport Jewish Discussion group. He also visited wounded troops in Liverpool hospitals, where the patients were only too happy to see a famous cricketer at their bedside. One such visit, to Childwall Hospital, provided him with one of the most emotional moments in his life, when some well chosen words that related his struggle with discrimination to the difficulties the men were facing in their newly limbless condition, were so well received with cheers that 'there was a lump in my throat and something like tears in my eyes'. Later he received a scroll signed by every patient at the hospital and he often talked of that experience as giving him more pleasure than anything he did in cricket.

The war also gave Constantine an entry into radio work, as he was enlisted by the government to broadcast to West Indians in the Caribbean on the contribution that their fellow countrymen were making to the war effort – as well as to file brief reports back 'home' on some of the cricket that was being played in Britain at the time. Constantine's easy style was well received, and as a result he was given an unscripted half hour slot on the BBC to talk to British listeners about his life in England. The programme received critical acclaim: the *Scotsman* newspaper, impressed with Constantine's 'rich musical voice', described the programme as 'one of the most impressive and effective ever from Broadcasting House', adding that 'the speaker told, without a word of bitterness, of the treatment he and his family had received in different parts of England ... on account of his colour. It was calculated to evoke shame or sympathy in equal measure'. The broadcast led to guest appearances, beginning in 1943, on the BBC's hugely popular wartime *Brains Trust* show, which regularly commanded audiences of 11 million or more. A forerunner of *Any Questions*, the programme invited distinguished panel members to air their views on topical questions and allowed Constantine, for the first time in such a high profile public forum, to put forward some of his left leaning views on race and self-government in the West Indies. It also provided the first indication that he would soon join the ranks of the 'great and the good' who so often made up such panels.

In October 1942 Constantine presented a radio programme on the Home service on calypso, and in September 1943 he fronted a 20-minute film documentary called *West Indies Calling* (also known as *Hallo West Indies*, and re-released as an item of cultural and historical interest in 2003) alongside the black writer and broadcaster Una Marson and Squadron Leader Ulric Cross, a highly decorated black airman. Essentially a propaganda tool for consumption in the West Indies, it looked at the wartime role of Caribbean men and women in the forces, factories, hospitals and on the land, and was based around conversations with West Indians who had gathered at Broadcasting House in London to describe their lives. The film, his talks, his welfare work and his entry into the politics of race took Constantine well away from his previous one-track professional life of cricket, cricket and more cricket.

His involvement with the game did not stop completely, however. Constantine played with success – and enjoyment – on Saturdays for the Yorkshire club Windhill in the Bradford League during 1940 and 1941, at a fee of £25 a match. When he left Windhill to take up his Welfare Officer job, he played when he could in the Liverpool and District League as an amateur and scored a typically bright century for a League XI against a Yorkshire XI in aid of the Red Cross – a match that included Len Hutton and Herbert Sutcliffe. He also appeared occasionally as an amateur for Nelson in 1942, the year his father died. Throughout the rest of the war he appeared in a string of charity matches, playing for – and often captaining – various makeshift and representative elevens, including a team of West Indians and Africans called The All Blacks, a British Empire XI, the Dominions and a number of West Indies XIs. Often these fixtures, typically in aid of the Red Cross or a hospital fund, would attract cricket starved crowds of up to 10,000, and a West Indies XI fixture against an All England team in the summer of 1943 was held at Lord's in front of 20,000. Being a major draw and crowd pleaser, Constantine was in constant demand for such matches in the summer, travelling many miles and raising many thousands of pounds in the process, but often refusing even to accept expenses. Just as often he would take the opportunity, after a game, to address the assembled spectators with one of his short speeches, peppered with jokes, about the Caribbean contribution to the war. He still loved playing cricket, but on top of his war work, and given that his fitness was at last failing, such

With the West Indies team at Lord's, 1939 (second from right)

matches were often draining affairs. In his prime on match days he would eat an orange or two for breakfast, take a little fish for lunch and then would eat 'a good meal when the day's work is done'. For many years he had kept his body in permanently good shape through a combination of watchful diet, three mile jogs at home, some modest weight lifting and abstinence from drink. But during the war he relaxed and would drink wine in moderation. While his performances were rarely as dominant as they had been before the war, the public were still prepared to show their appreciation. His assistant at the ministry of Labour, Sam Morris, told of one such wartime match when a packed crowd gave Constantine a huge reception on his way to the wicket and an even bigger one on his way back to the pavilion, even though he had been out first ball for 0. 'The look of incredulity on the face of the bowler was shattering. One could sense his sorrow at what he, or rather the ball, had done, and one felt he wished the cricket laws could be bent to allow Constantine another go. There was a momentary hush among the crowd, but as Constantine continued to walk back to the pavilion less than two minutes after he had left it, the ovation he received was greater than the reception he had going in to bat. The spontaneous ovation was not for cricketing achievement on that day, but for the tremendous all round reputation that he had already built up in this country.'

Constantine also played his last first class match in August 1945 when, just short of 44, he was appointed captain of a Dominions team composed, apart from himself, of white Australian, New Zealand and South African cricketers in a high profile and exciting three-day match against England at Lord's. Although he had been given the honour of the captaincy by Plum Warner, Warner had run the idea past all the other players and they were more than happy with his choice. Much to Constantine's satisfaction, given that this was the highest profile captaincy of his career, he skippered the side to victory with just eight minutes to spare. He executed an audacious trademark run out and put on a fine 123-run partnership (of which he made 40) with the Australian Keith Miller. But otherwise Constantine made only a limited impact with bat or ball and, in an observation that acknowledged not just the muted atmosphere of a sporting contest in the throes of war but also his own waning powers, he noted that: 'There was the old familiar murmur from the crowd as I went to the wicket, followed by the same electric silence; the fielders spread out in the old remembered way; but there was not the sparkle or the exhilaration in it as of old'. Cricket was still an important part of Constantine's life, even though it no longer brought him a significant income.

But it was rapidly taking a back seat to other priorities – notably the fight against racial prejudice. There could have been no better illustration of this new reality than in the run-up to Constantine's high profile two-day game for the Dominions against England at Lord's in early August 1943, when his preparations for the match had been overshadowed by an unsavoury incident that led to a landmark legal case which helped define the future shape of legislation on racial discrimination in Britain.

Constantine had booked himself, Norma and Gloria into London's Imperial Hotel for four nights around the big match, but when the family arrived on 30 July 1943 they were told they could have a room for just one night and would have to go elsewhere for the duration of their stay as their presence might offend other guests. It was not the first time Constantine had been refused hotel accommodation or a table at a restaurant on account of his skin colour. Apart from a number of incidents in which he had been directly involved, he also knew that his friend, the black actor and singer Paul Robeson, had been barred from London's Savoy Hotel in 1930, and on another occasion he had tried, in vain, to help a British company find hotel spaces for some visiting black West Indian businessmen. But Constantine found the Imperial Hotel incident particularly bruising because it had impinged on his wife and daughter rather than just himself. He was also especially upset because he was in London to represent the Dominions, and, despite his liberal, left-leaning politics, he was a supporter of the spirit of the British Empire in as much as it had the potential to bring together races from around the world in a common purpose and with common bonds – not least in war and sport. The fact that he could be seen on the one hand as a proud public representative of that Commonwealth, yet, behind the scenes, regarded as not worthy even to stay in the same accommodation as whites, angered and disappointed him. Given the new freedom he now felt to delve into racial matters, Constantine decided to draw a line in the sand. He initiated legal action against the Imperial Hotel.

The case of *Constantine v Imperial London Hotels* came to court a year later in June 1944 in front of Mr Justice Birkett, partly coinciding with another appearance by Constantine at Lord's, this time as captain of a West Indies XI playing an England XI. Constantine was represented in court by two prominent figures – Sir Patrick Hastings, a former Labour MP and attorney general who had also represented Sir Oswald Mosley on several occasions when he was prosecuted for public order offences as leader of the British Union of Fascists, and Rose Heilbron, the first woman in Britain to become a barrister.

As there was no specific legislation in Britain to prevent racial discrimination in the provision of services, the case was brought on the basis of a breach of contract by the hotel. Constantine told the court that he had telephoned the Imperial in advance to book the room and, as a precaution learnt from bitter experience, had informed the manager that he was black. When he was assured that this was no problem, he went ahead with the booking and paid a £2 deposit. But on the day he and his family arrived, the management's demeanour had changed significantly, mainly because there was now a large contingent of white American army officers staying in the hotel.

The hotel's manageress felt the presence of a black family might upset the American soldiers, who were still used to segregation back home. There was also a suggestion that she had received complaints from some parties as soon as Constantine's entourage had walked through the door.

When Constantine arrived at the reception desk with a colleague from the Ministry of Labour (probably Sam Morris), he signed the register and went up to his room. However, he was swiftly informed by a porter that he was required to come back down urgently to speak to the management. While he had been upstairs, his work colleague had been told by the manageress that 'we will not have niggers in the hotel because of the Americans', and that although the family would be allowed to stay the night 'their luggage will be put out tomorrow and the doors locked'. A row ensued, during which the man from the ministry pointed out that Constantine was a civil servant and a British subject. The manageress replied that he was 'still a nigger'. Although indignant, Constantine was persuaded by his work colleague – and perhaps by the presence of his wife and daughter – to take an alternative offer of a four-night stay at the nearby Bedford Hotel, owned by the same company but not, on this occasion, full of American soldiers.

The defence argued that even though the company had refused Constantine accommodation at the Imperial Hotel, he had left voluntarily and it had performed its obligation in common law by putting him and his family up at the Bedford Hotel. However, Justice Birkett ruled that the move to the Bedford was 'of no matter', that the company had sufficient room to receive him at the Imperial, that Constantine 'was a man of high character' and that 'although he was a man of colour, no ground existed on which the defendants were entitled to refuse to receive and lodge him at the hotel'.

Birkett praised Constantine for behaving with 'modesty and dignity' both at the time of the incident and in the courtroom, where his evidence was generally regarded as erudite and impressive. He ruled that Constantine had 'suffered much unjustifiable humiliation and distress' and found in his favour, awarding damages of five guineas. Although, for technical reasons, the award was nominal only – and less than he would have received from a collection for scoring a 50 in a league match – Constantine emerged as a clear and popular victor, receiving a large mail bag of hundreds of congratulatory letters after his win. While he felt he could have gone on to pursue the hotel for more money in a defamation action, he was content to have raised the issue so prominently in the public eye, and to leave it at that. Typically, he claimed not to have taken the case to assuage any personal hurt but 'to draw the particular nature of the affront before the wider judgment of the British public, in the hope that its sense of fair play might help to protect people of my colour in England in future'. The fact that he was a well known and popular figure leant the case a prominence it may not have gained had it involved an 'ordinary' black person during wartime. Newspaper coverage had been copious, and the matter had even prompted questions in the House of Commons. Thanks partly to his employment at the Ministry of Labour, Constantine also had the government's support. Constantine was the first person to challenge the colour bar in the British courts in this way. The case did not end racial discrimination in West End hotels or restaurants, but it did put a brake on such practices, and as Constantine had intended, laid down some kind of marker. *Constantine v Imperial London Hotels* is still seen as a historic moment in the British battle for race equality, as it demonstrated that although a black person could not prosecute for discrimination on racial grounds, he or she could go to court to claim damages for personal distress and injury. It also neatly exposed the fact that there was no specific

First among equals: examining the Lord's pitch with England captain Walter Hammond prior to the 1944 England XI v West Indies match

legislation that prohibited discrimination in services or jobs on the basis of race, and as such was one of the key milestones along the road to the creation of the Race Relations Act of 1965. And it presaged a new willingness by black people to challenge the status quo. The historian of British black history, Peter Fryer, described Constantine's victory as 'a turning point in the struggle against one of the most pernicious forms of colour bar in Britain'. For Constantine personally it was an event that came to be associated with him in Britain as much as anything he did on the cricket field – and marked him out as a campaigner on race issues. He was to continue the theme after 1945 as he exploited the wartime base he had established in broadcasting to re-establish his legal credentials and to move ever more into the field of politics.

5 Civilian life

The immediate post-war period allowed Constantine, at last, to spend a great deal more time with his wife. The full-time cricketing years had taken him from Nelson on many occasions, and his war work – based as it was in Liverpool – had kept him from seeing as much of Norma as he would have liked. Gloria had progressed from Nelson Grammar School to St Andrew's University in Scotland, and with the time and space now to concentrate on his own affairs, Constantine once again set his sights on the legal profession. He knew that an intense period of home study lay ahead, and that he would have to generate money to pay for those studies in a way that would, ideally, give him freedom to put in the academic hours.

Initially that meant a return to Windhill Cricket Club in the Bradford League, who were still willing to offer Constantine decent money as their professional, despite the fact that he was now in his mid forties. He had accepted that his serious cricketing days were over, but found the offer of a contract for the 1946 season too tempting to resist. He also landed a weekday coaching job in Dublin during the summer of 1946 and accepted the post with alacrity, not least because Ireland was free from rationing and he was keen to sample some good food after years of war time restrictions. His popularity as a coach serving Trinity College, Dublin, Leinster Cricket Club and St Mary's College suggested he could have earned a good living in the field, but it was not an avenue he seemed keen to fully explore – although he did later spend three months coaching and playing in Ceylon (now Sri Lanka) during 1953, when Norma went along with him. He also played some cricket in Scotland immediately after the war for the Colonial Cricket Club, a team of West Indian residents in Edinburgh. But his main cricketing work was with Windhill during the years 1946, 1947 and 1948 – topping the Bradford League bowling averages in his last two seasons. When the time came to end his league career, against Keighley, he marked his final appearance in suitably dramatic fashion – taking a wicket off the last ball he bowled and then, with a victory needed to secure the title for his club, scoring a whirlwind 69 not out that ended with a match-winning four 'that went humming to the boundary as clean as any ball I have ever hit'.

Cricket was a useful post-war stop-gap, but it was no longer Constantine's future. When it came to providing a good income with the flexibility to study, broadcasting and print journalism seemed to fit the bill. Building on the start he had made in the war, Constantine began by filing match reports, Test match previews, background articles and opinion pieces for the Reuters news agency, whose sports editor, Vernon Morgan, had approached him to cover the 1946 Indian tour of England for a total fee of £200. Eager to take up such an attractive offer, Constantine had written to the Ministry of Labour asking if he could have his leave entitlement of two and a half days per month plus extra leave without pay until his job was expected to end in June 1946. Permission was granted. Constantine could write well enough, and was a proficient typist – a legacy of his days as a clerk – but he was primarily chosen for his famous name and his insights. In the early days he was shadowed by the journalist Frank Stuart, who would tidy up his copy, help him meet deadlines, and even ghost-write some pieces. Nonetheless, Constantine caught on quick, and made a big impression on the press corps when he arrived on the scene. At the Lord's Test between England and India in June 1946, according to one newspaper man who was present, 'he reduced the press box to respectful silence in a few minutes by the acuteness and originality of his remarks about what was going on out in the middle. He was not only a man who played the game really well – he understood it really well too, and every department of it. I have never in my life listened to such an illuminating and impromptu running commentary'. CLR James, himself a successful cricket reporter, had always felt that Constantine had the makings of a good commentator on the game; he was perceptive and astute, but never willing to use his status as a first class player to dismiss the thoughts of those who had not been out in the middle. 'Constantine was always ready to argue and never used the argument that he had been there and we were only spectators,' he said.

During the period immediately after the war, Constantine also wrote four cricket books. The first of them, the autobiographical *Cricket in the Sun*, published in 1947 by Stanley Paul, went back over much of the ground he had covered in his first, 1933 book, *Cricket and I*, but also took up the story to the end of his first class career. The most engaging of the seven books he wrote or co-wrote, it also aired more of his views on race and alluded to some of the racial snubs he had encountered during his cricketing life – though not at any great length. Constantine did not mince his words in print, accusing the reactionary MCC stalwart Lord Hawke of being 'Hitlerian', but he also displayed an engaging, often humorous, writing style, and the book opened with the memorable lines: "Trinidad was discovered by Columbus in 1496, and by the MCC in 1895. I came on the scene as a pickaninny in 1920 and discovered England in 1923, when I came over with a West Indies cricket team. Improving on Columbus, I settled down to make the most of my discovery....' Firmly against the trend of bland cricketing reminiscences, *Cricket in the Sun* was an outspoken volume, raising not just the issue of racism but savagely criticizing anything Constantine saw as getting in the way of the game he loved – including the old order of gentlemen and players, slow play, those who criticized short pitched bowling and the undervaluing of fielding. Although he had a tendency, like many old players, to hark back to the better days of his prime, he was also unusually forward looking and not afraid to suggest radical ideas such as the use of four umpires, time limits on batsmen that would see them given out if they did not score to a set rate against the clock, and, most presciently of all, a World Cup of one-day cricket. Money was important to him, and he talked about it openly in his books, detailing his pay in the leagues and for the West Indies, which was again an unusual stance.

Three more straightforward cricketing books followed in short order: *Cricketers' Carnival* (1948), a rather self indulgent book based around his imaginings of a match between two teams of his favourite cricketers; *Cricket Crackers* (1949), largely given over to his thoughts on various aspects and controversies of the

On the dinner circuit: Constantine holds forth at a 1950 event attended by long-time acquaintance Neville Cardus (third from left), with whom he had originally put CLR James in contact

game, and *Cricketers' Cricket* (also 1949), an extended coaching manual with tips on how to master the arts of bowling, batting and fielding. Quite unexpectedly, *Cricketer's Cricket* finished, in a final chapter on the future of the game, with some words that revealed the hidden depths of his inner worries at the time. Referring to the 'obstinate will' of the conservative cricketing establishment, Constantine complained that their desire to hold back the hands of time was 'a symbol of the failing intelligence of the Western

World, clinging to its wars and inequalities, its racial barriers and shibboleths, and its hopelessly unstable and toppling financial and political framework within which the little people, who only want to be left alone to enjoy their cricket quietly, are conscripted and directed and badgered and taxed and slain, and hypnotized by yelling newspapers and yodelling political gang-leaders to slay one another faster and faster in a maniac's saraban, without reason, rhyme or law'. It was a breathless, apocalyptic and rather disturbing way to round off an otherwise straightforward book on cricket coaching, but typical of the Constantine view, espoused in *Cricket in the Sun*, that 'I do not see why I must be conventional in writing any more than in batting'.

Freed now from the restraints he had imposed on himself as a cricketer ('I hold views about politics, but so far as I know I have never aired them while I have been wearing flannels'), Constantine used his books to reveal some of the personal stories of racism that had impinged on his private and professional life. In *Cricket in the Sun* he disclosed, for the first time, that he and other black players in the West Indies side had been upset for many years by the practice in the islands of holding social functions for MCC tourists – usually dances – that were for whites only. Often these were arranged behind the scenes to minimize embarrassment, but in Jamaica he recalled that the organizers would make it 'deliberately and painfully clear' to the black players that they were not wanted at such functions. 'I recall [England's] Jack Iddon talking to me at a dinner and saying; "I'll see you at the dance later". I am sure many English players remain in ignorance of what happens, just as he did, for not only had I not been invited to that dance, I had never even heard of it,' he said. Constantine generally maintained that, in cricket at least, he had experienced far less racial tension in England than in the West Indies – and less still in league cricket compared with the first class game. Just 'once or twice' he encountered problems in the league, which he documented freely in his books. One such occasion involved Jimmy Blanckenberg, the South African pace bowler, who was professional for East Lancashire when Constantine played against him for Nelson. When Constantine went up to Blanckenberg to offer his greetings before the match 'he turned his back on me very obviously'. Constantine responded with an extremely hostile spell of fast bowling at his opposite number. 'After the match there were two black men, for Blanckenberg had some ripe bruises,' he laughed. 'He did not like the colour of his skin any better than mine, for he came to our dressing room and said loudly to our captain: "look what your blinking professional has done to me!" This made several people laugh, though I was very grave.' Blanckenberg also complained to the Nelson committee, and while its members backed their own professional, Constantine subsequently fell out with one club member over the issue.

On another occasion, when the wife of an (unnamed) Australian cricketer visited Nelson to watch Constantine's first league match in 1929, she created a fuss about not wanting to meet Constantine or his wife, and there was 'an atmosphere' for which the club chairman later apologized. Off the field at a 'famous cricket gathering' a white guest had said aloud to another as Norma approached them: 'I see they've let the jungle in on us'.

At other times Constantine felt the hand of prejudice had been at work when he received personal criticisms from various quarters – not least when he was occasionally accused of being an overpaid mercenary. He was also convinced, as he related in *Cricket in the Sun*, that Lancashire County Cricket Club's initial interest in signing him as a professional around 1934 was blocked by racism on the county's committee. Although Constantine maintained that he had the support of the Lancashire club chairman, and had been privately approached to see if he would consider such an offer, the idea never reached full committee. 'I was told that whatever my cricket, certain influential people on the Lancashire board could not tolerate my colour,' he said.

Constantine was often disarmingly dismissive of the personal hurt that such slights brought him, preferring instead to focus on how similar acts of prejudice more deeply affected other black people less fortunate than himself. When, before the war, he had taken up his complaint at Rochdale about the racial abuse he received from an umpire, he did so, he said, 'not because I needed any personal protection from such behaviour, as I have shown on other occasions that I can take care of myself', but because 'there were several coloured players in the Lancashire clubs at the time, among them some West Indians, and not all of them were so financially and otherwise able as I was to risk the ... action'. Not the least of these was his brother Elias. On a personal level, Constantine often preferred to direct his anger into his game. 'You would be surprised if you knew how many sixes had sailed in how many different directions simply because, at that moment, I was fiercely resenting some sorrow of my race,' he confided.

As the contents of Constantine's post-war books came largely from his head and required little research, they could have been rattled off at fairly rapid speed on his typewriter, especially as he may have had some ghost writing help along the way. But given the extent of Constantine's other writing and broadcasting work, plus his continuing cricketing commitments and studies, he generated a prodigious output across such a short period. This partly helped him pay for the not insubstantial expenses he was accruing through his legal studies – as did a cricket coaching cartoon series under his name in *Eagle* magazine and his own autograph branded bat, made and sold by Walter Lambert & Sons.

Although Constantine did well in print – as author, columnist and reporter – his real forte was in radio broadcasting. When the West Indies came to England for their 1950 tour he commentated for the BBC on all the Test matches, earning around £300 in the summer and witnessing, to his great delight, the West Indies' first victory at Lord's, immortalized in the Lord Beginner calypso *Cricket Lovely Cricket*. The most famous lines of that song, 'with those little pals of mine, Ramadhin and Valentine' had been adapted from a much earlier Beginner composition that celebrated Constantine's 1928 touring feats with the line: 'Learie Constantine, that old pal of mine'.

Expertly tutored by the all round sports commentator Rex Alston, Constantine had a quiet, relaxed broadcasting voice, described as 'sincere and unaffected' by his BBC bosses in a private memo. The great radio man and writer John Arlott, with whom he worked on cricket broadcasts after the war, found him 'an extremely good natural broadcaster' who was 'simple and direct' and 'never embarked on involved constructions' when describing the action in front of him. He was soon in much demand for a range of other broadcasts, including *Women's Hour*, schools and children's programmes and anything to do with the Commonwealth or the West Indies. Constantine enjoyed broadcasting; it suited his outgoing temperament and his love of talking, and it paid well, which was always an important consideration for him.

Given his many years of making impromptu speeches at cricket matches and in town halls, he was often at his best when

Achievement for achievement's sake?: Constantine was eventually called to the bar, but had little time to practise the profession

improvising or speaking without a prepared script, and would occasionally diverge from a prepared script in any case – sometimes to the exasperation of his producers. A naturally proficient and occasionally stylish writer, the scripts he typed up for himself rarely needed editing, although they were sometimes loose with the facts. He was most popular and accomplished when talking about his personal experiences in Trinidad and Britain, about his early life in the Caribbean, his dominant time in the leagues or his unusual job during the war. In the immediate post-war period before the beginning of mass West Indian immigration to Britain, such broadcasts were intriguing for British audiences largely ignorant of the Caribbean or the people who lived there – and Constantine invited sympathy for his position and causes. When the narrative strayed into polemic, however, he was occasionally accused of over-egging his case. 'He was at his best as a narrator, but less effective when he was the persuader,' said Gerald Howat, who listened to many of his broadcasts. 'His persuasive passages invited his listeners to sympathize with him in a situation – usually a racial one. But he was apt to be long-winded in his determination to establish his views.'

Broadcasting, which was always occasional rather than full-time, gave Constantine the time and money to pursue his legal studies. But it also acted as an antidote to the slog of studying, which he found a less natural pursuit. His dogged pursuit of legal qualifications had about it a whiff of achievement for achievement's sake – there is little sense that he especially enjoyed the subject matter or the profession itself, and when he eventually qualified he was to practise in law for only a handful of years – and even then intermittently. He applied himself with grim determination to his studies rather than with the smiling gusto he reserved for any other task of his choosing. It was a tough ask for a man who, as Denzil Batchelor observed, wore life 'like a flamboyant tie'. CLR James, among others, recognized that status was important to the self-made Constantine, who despite his cricketing achievements and relative financial security, still felt slightly naked without any qualifications. He resented the fact that he had been unable to progress far in his Trinidadian law clerk jobs – notwithstanding his underlying desire to be a cricketer – and was determined to prove to himself, and others, that only circumstances had prevented him from moving up the ladder. He also saw that a grounding in law could be a stepping stone to other things.

Constantine had laid the ground for his post-war studies in 1944 by entering himself as a law student with one of the four London Inns of Court, the Middle Temple. From 1946 onwards this allowed him to set out on the painful road towards bar examinations in the chambers of the barrister Gerald Hart. Although he did receive tutorials in London, most of Constantine's early study involved poring over books at home when his broadcasting and writing work allowed, which was not easy for someone who had not studied for the best part of 30 years and was such a gregarious personality. Here Norma became an important driving force, intervening to curb his lively home-based social life, which after the war had quickly become an endless whirl of calling friends and impromptu evenings around the dinner table. Personal papers show that people from all walks of life were eager to make and retain Constantine's acquaintance, to ask for his help or seek his attention. He was careful with money but generous with it too, giving large sums privately (and with no fuss) not only to charities but to a string of mainly West Indian suitors who approached him for financial help. He saw this as one way in which he could help the West Indian community in Britain, even if it left him exposed to risk. Surviving personal papers show that at one time he almost certainly lost a significant sum of money when he bailed out a prominent West Indian restaurateur whose business continued to fail, leaving him unable to pay back the 'loan' from Constantine.

Constantine was also perhaps overly generous with his private time and, according to Norma, was not always able to distinguish the self-serving hangers-on from those who had more to offer him personally. On the other hand he was not afraid of breaking up valued friendships if necessary, as surviving correspondence between himself and his erstwhile West Indies bowling companion Manny Martindale attests. Martindale, a Barbadian who lived in Burnley and played in the leagues too, had a bitter falling out with Constantine. This was partly over the fact that the former had appeared to use Constantine's pay negotiations during the 1939 Test series to hold out for extra money himself, partly due to what Constantine perceived as Martindale's easy-come-easy-go attitude to their friendship. The often vituperative correspondence, in which Constantine gave as good as he got, showed a hard-edged side to him that was rarely revealed.

Fairly soon after Constantine's home studies began, Norma and Gloria decided to keep a count of the number of visitors to the house – and gave up after reaching 100 people in a three-week spell. Norma drew the line, reducing the number of sanctioned visitors to virtually none, while, according to her later (and probably apocryphal) recall, she literally locked her restless husband into his bedroom for seven hour days of concerted studying. He had moved past the first landmark by 1947, when he passed his exams on Roman Law, but the pace was hardly swift. James, now living in the United States, often scoured the newspapers to see if his friend had passed the finishing line. He failed to see anything for a number of years. On many occasions Constantine was close to defeat, but he kept up the struggle by dint of Norma's insistence and his own innate determination. He was also driven by the conviction that becoming a barrister was the best way of executing a meaningful return to Trinidad.

Constantine had considered another route home, but it had come to naught. In early 1947, having noted Constantine's successful war time efforts as a Welfare Officer, his old employers, Trinidad Leaseholds, had approached him with an attractive offer to become a liaison officer. This would have involved him working to smooth the increasingly strained relations between black workers and white managers at the company's headquarters in southern Trinidad. On paper it was an interesting and challenging job – and it came with a 'fine four figure salary' plus a number of perks, including a role in promoting and coaching cricket. Constantine sailed to Trinidad to find out more. When he got there, however, he soon became nervous about the path that had been mapped out for him. A month on reconnaissance showed him that his employers essentially wanted him to keep things quiet rather than to promote any meaningful dialogue or change. 'My popularity as a cricketer was to be used to dissuade coloured rebelliousness … whether it was right or wrong,' he said later. 'Numbers of the coloured workers had reached a stage where they were uncertain of their white controllers, so I, a coloured man whom they liked because I had knocked a few sixes over the palm trees, was to come in to tell them not to be impatient, that really everything was being done for their good.' This was not the progressive role Constantine had envisaged, nor was it to take place in an environment that had especially changed for the better since he had left the company 19 years before. As evidence that the old colour consciousness remained, he was subjected to a chastening snub when an invite to eat in the company's exclusive senior staff dining club was hastily withdrawn – under a flimsy pretext – after a white employee, or employees, had clearly made unfavourable noises about his imminent presence.

In the end Constantine declined the job offer, although he was greatly tempted by a return to Trinidad and 'burning to show what I could do for good in my own land'. In a broadcast on the BBC in 1945 he had said he wanted 'to work for my people: work in the field of education and quicken progress to the goal of self-reliance and self-government'. Although he admitted to being 'confused' as to how he should actually do this, the Trinidad Leaseholds offer had momentarily suggested one avenue. Reluctantly he concluded that he should continue studying law in England in the hope that he could come back to Trinidad on better terms at some point in the future.

So it was that legal studies loomed large in Constantine's life for the eight years after the war. In 1949 he and Norma made the decision to move down to London, where he would be nearer the inns of court for tutorials as well as much of his broadcasting and writing work. In July they ended the rental agreement on their home in Meredith Street in Nelson and moved into a flat at 101 Lexham Gardens in Earls Court, west London. Although it was a logical move, especially now that Gloria had graduated from St Andrew's University and was embarking on teacher training at the University of London's Institute of Education, it was a sad leaving of the town after 20 years, both for the family and the townsfolk. Nelson retained a special place in Constantine's heart.

The move to London was at least a decisive break away from the rigours of serious league cricket, but he continued to play for fun down south whenever he felt able, most notably for the Buckinghamshire village of Chalfont St Peter, where fellow players were struck by his habit of never taking tea between innings so that he could spend the entire break coaching the local youngsters.

While he studied, wrote and broadcast, Constantine also continued his role in the politics of race, even using his farewell speech to the Nelson Methodists to raise the topic. In 1947 he had become chairman of the League of Coloured Peoples following the death of Harold Moody, and he sat on the organization's executive committee with Hastings Banda, a UK-based GP who was later to become the first President of Malawi. But Moody was the driving force behind the League, and without him its influence began to wane. Despite Constantine's best efforts, the organization had never boasted a big membership – several hundred people at most – and he could not arrest its decline. It folded in 1951. At some point around this time Constantine was also approached to help organize a black Olympic games in Liberia, although the venture came to nothing. This was as a result, he claimed, of interference by the Americans, who effectively exercised control over the country and did not want 'to allow the place to become a demonstration ground to show that coloured organizers can make a success of anything'. Constantine was elected president of the London branch of the Caribbean Labour Congress, a trade union body, in 1948, hosting meetings and talks on politics and labour problems in the Caribbean. He also served as a member of the Colonial Office's Colonial Social Welfare Advisory Committee for three years up to 1950. In that same year he became deeply involved in the Seretse Kharma affair, pitting himself against the Labour government of Clement Attlee. Kharma, an English educated Chieftain of the Barmangwato people in the Bechuanaland Protectorate of South Africa, had upset the racist South African authorities by marrying a white English woman, Ruth William. Under pressure from South African officials, the British government, which could easily have ignored the fuss, summoned Kharma to London on what

Kharma later claimed were false pretences. When he arrived he was told that he would no longer be recognized as chief and was barred from returning. An outraged Constantine helped to form the Seretse Kharma Fighting Committee, of which he was chairman, to push for Kharma's return and reinstatement. Although Kharma eventually became the first President of Botswana, Constantine's lobbying over the affair was unsuccessful at the time, and Kharma and his wife decided to stay in England on a government grant. Constantine, though he liked Kharma, felt he should have refused the money, 'worked for a living, and stood by his rights'. The affair kept Constantine in the public eye over the issue of racism as he organized public meetings, parliamentary lobbying and appeals to the United Nations. But it added to his frustration at what he felt was a general lack of interest from the Labour government in racial issues. 'We might as well just have whistled to the wind in any matter where black and white politics were concerned,' he said. Constantine was disappointed by Attlee's apparent blind spot on race, claiming, on the basis of personal meetings with him, that he 'seemed to feel a sense of white superiority over coloured people and their affairs'. While he may have spent much of his time in England in the orbit of the Labour Party and appeared to be broadly in tune with its welfare policies, Constantine was by no means a staunch supporter of the party, partly because his prime concern was racial, rather than party politics, partly because the Liberal Party's take on race was more in line with his own. Gloria recalls emphatically that her father's politics 'were Labour', but he was not at heart a joiner, and often maintained a certain distance from the political process. He was never dogmatic in his views and did not subscribe to a fixed set of ideological positions. In the same year as the Kharma affair, Constantine was invited to stand in the general election as a Liberal candidate for Shipley in Yorkshire against Arthur Creech-Jones, who had been Secretary of State for the Colonies in the Labour government. 'I considered the possibilities, and finally refused, since I did not think I could help coloured people in that way,' he said. In fact Creech-Jones lost his seat, so it was possible that Constantine might have won. But he had little desire to be an MP; he believed his most effective role, in Britain at least, could be built by influencing through example and commentary rather than through direct political action. He felt he could be more influential in the wider public sphere.

By the time of the Liberal Party's approach, Constantine was also at last making steady headway in the various parts of his bar exams. Although four more years of slog were to follow, his toil was finally rewarded, at the age of 53, when he was called to the bar by the Middle Temple in late 1954. He learned of his success while on a visit to Stockton, and the relief was immense. 'I am very pleased,' he told the *Northern Echo* newspaper. 'That is putting it mildly, but the Englishman is famous for his understatements and I have lived among you long enough to absorb your customs.' The *Nelson Leader* ran the news under the headline 'Local boy makes good'.

His new status as a barrister at law allowed him, at last, to put into action his long-held plan to return to Trinidad. Earlier in the year he had received another offer from his old employer, Trinidad Leaseholds – by now merged with Texaco – to take up a senior post, once he was qualified, as the company's assistant legal adviser on £700 a year. With change fomenting in his homeland and Gloria (now a schoolteacher) set for a Port of Spain marriage to the Trinidadian barrister Andre Valere, whom she had met in

London, it was a fitting and exciting time to go home. He accepted the offer.

The job at Trinidad Leaseholds provided Constantine with the return to Trinidad he had dreamed about for some time, but it was not without its possible drawbacks. He had lived in England for a quarter of a century, and was settled there. He knew, too, that he was now a valued member of British society. There was no guarantee of such a place in his homeland, where the racial barriers that had blocked his progress so many years before were still firmly in place – and where his absence had not necessarily made the hearts of the people grow fonder. 'My heart was in my boots,' he later admitted. 'I felt like someone emigrating rather than someone returning home. I was not looking forward to the restrictive atmosphere of Trinidad – a colony where the white man held most of the power, made most of the money and kept pretty well to himself.'

Despite these misgivings, and as he made preparations for the boat journey to Trinidad, Constantine left Britain with a distinctly thorny going-away present. It was a fifth book, this time vastly different from any he had written before, and it was anything but a gift-wrapped offering designed to leave his second home in good humour. *Colour Bar* (1954), which he had written with his journalistic collaborator Frank Stuart over the previous couple of years – despite being in the throes of his bar exams – was a parting shot that left no one in any doubt as to the strength of his feelings on race relations in Britain and the world beyond. It's first sentence was: 'I am black.'

Colour Bar was Constantine's first – and only – literary launch into the heart of the issue of racial politics, but it was a definitive one. He claimed he had been urged to write the book by white journalists who thought he should expand on some of his experiences of racism and to set out his views on the way forward. There was plenty of interest in his standpoint, but the contents must have come as an unpleasant surprise to those who had seen Constantine as a largely benign black presence in Britain. The United Kingdom, he wrote, was 'only a little less intolerant' than segregated America or South Africa. Although he had made 'innumerable white friends' in Britain, 'I still think it would be just to say that almost the entire population of Britain really expects the coloured man to live in an inferior area devoted to coloured people, and not to have free and open choice of a living place. Most British people would be quite unwilling for a black man to enter their homes, nor would they wish to work with one as a colleague, nor to stand shoulder to shoulder with one at a factory bench. Hardly any Englishwomen and not more than a small proportion of Englishmen would sit at a restaurant table with a coloured man or woman, and inter-racial marriage is considered almost universally to be out of the question.'

The short-sighted behaviour of Britons on the wider stage also came in for scathing criticism, with the country's colonial policy in countries such as Kenya and British Guiana characterized as 'let sleeping dogs lie till they rise and bite, then shoot them'. Britain's willful neglect of the human rights of its black subjects abroad, he wrote, 'costs first fortunes of the taxpayers' money, then the lives of coloured "natives" and white conscripts, and finally the loss of the colony'. He went on: 'The excuse is always: "The African is not ready for responsibility." But nothing is done to make him ready, everything is done to prevent the majority of Africans from making themselves ready. A bright boy here and there is picked out and part-educated – but only if he is docile and obedient to white control, and these boys are vetted for lower-grade leadership strictly in white leadings-strings.' He even criticized the Queen – a bold move in such times – for not inviting a single black person to a state dinner in Bermuda despite the fact that 'most of her people there are coloured', adding that 'however misled the people of Britain may be over Commonwealth matters and however they are made to think that the Christmas broadcast is an unbiased picture of a completely happy empire, the rest of the world is under no such delusions'.

Much of the 193-page book was a guided tour through racial oppression around the world, cataloguing injustices in the deep south of America, South Africa, colonial Africa and India. It also devoted many pages to countering 'nonsense' theories of innate racial inferiority. And it laid out a broad manifesto for progress – universal suffrage, black majority rule, trade union recognition, redistribution of land, the building of millions of new houses, and free child and adult education programmes. However, it was the personal revelations in *Colour Bar* that were the most significant, for the book was far more of a call for white action than it was a call to arms for black people. Written specifically with a white British audience in mind, indeed directly addressed to them, it went for the jugular as well as the heart strings. No one had yet opened up so personally or passionately to a British audience about the hurt of racial prejudice.

'How would it seem to you if we applied the lessons you have taught us?' he asked. 'If we shut you into reservations, kept you in slum ghettoes in towns, taught our children to shout at white ayahs and white houseboys, kicked your white rulers off their thrones for asking questions and replaced them with pro-black regents? It is hard to make it understood by white people how much we resent

– and fear – this perpetual undercurrent of jeering, this ingrained belief in the white mind that the coloured man, woman or child is a matter for mirth or – at the very best – a kind of devoted, loyal dog to a white all-powerful master, the Kipling conception. Rather than be everlastingly sniggered at, we would almost rather be lynched!'

Constantine had kept a reasonably tight lid on personal revelations of prejudice in his other books, but they were allowed free rein in *Colour Bar*. 'Like most other coloured people, if I am introduced to a white person, I have learned now to keep my hand at my side until a white hand is plainly offered to me,' he confessed. 'A good many times of holding my hand out and having it ignored has taught me what I must call "Negro-in-England" manners.'

He recounted many stories of racist incidents, including the taxi driver who had told him 'I'm sick of seeing you bloody niggers with our white women' after giving a lift to Constantine and a 60-year-old female work colleague. He also told of an occasion in the dining compartment of a train from London to Manchester when he was directed by the stewards to a vacant seat at a table for two, where a white woman was sitting. 'I bowed to the lady, who ignored me,' he recalled. 'Then as I sat down opposite her, she leapt up and shouted, "Steward, get me another seat." The steward pointed out, most courteously, an obvious fact – there was not another vacant seat in the diner. "I'm afraid you'll have to wait, madam," he said. "I'm sorry." The lady waited, standing rigidly upright beside my table; and under those circumstances I had to eat my lunch. I don't know what I ate, and I was bitterly thankful to get out afterwards.'

This was the book Constantine had been threatening to write for many years, and he did not spare anyone's blushes. In the context of the mid-1950s it was an outspoken, challenging, hard hitting tome, the more so because it came not from a known black militant but from someone who seemed so charming, so unruffled, so suited to British society. While it preached non-violence, it warned that 'nothing and no-one will stop us' and made no bones about the fact that force would inevitably have to be used if change did not materialize. 'People who feel themselves oppressed come to violence in the end, just as a person in intolerable pain cannot keep still for ever,' he argued. Constantine admitted to feeling 'sick and savage for the rest of the day' when learning of some new outrage against black people around the world. The book contained a photograph of a black man being burned at the stake by an American mob; the book jacket conceded that its author was speaking with 'shocking frankness'.

Out of its 1950s context, *Colour Bar* may now, in some areas, appear simplistic – even gauche. It contains a series of illustrations with captions such as 'coloured people are intelligent too', and features an idiot's guide on how not to cause racial offence ('don't use the words "nigger", do not refer to "natives" or "darkeys", do not drop the Mr, Mrs, or Miss when referring to a black person'). It counters suggestions that black people exude an "animal" odour by stating that many white people 'give off an offensive "sour milk" smell, which Constantine has 'personally detected from an excited white crowd at a greyhound stadium and in a cotton mill in Lancashire on a hot day'. In an attempt to debunk the myth that black people are widely and sexually promiscuous, he argues that 'sex excitements are indulged in far more among poor people with less alternative entertainments and harder and more drab lives, whereas the higher in the social and intellectual scale the investigator ascends, the less interest in sex is shown'. Elsewhere he states that 'the American negro is culturally further forward than the African tribesman, the Indian than the Polynesian'.

Colour Bar is, however, a book of its time, and judged in that time it was an important contribution to the debate about race and colonialism. How much it improved race relations in Britain or hurried the end of empire is impossible to tell. But no black man in Britain had written a book quite like it: such a mix of personal memoir and political thought. And because of Constantine's currency in British society it reached a wide audience. While *Colour Bar* may not have done much to energize the black masses or even the black intelligentsia (it did not, for instance, appear to particularly impress CLR James, who felt it had 'bowled a few wides and quite a few no balls'). But it was a significant shot across the bows of the white man on the street, and it established Constantine as a major black spokesman. It also marked him out as a man who, while viewed in some circles as a relatively conservative campaigner on race, was actually a radical Pan-Africanist, a man who saw the personal difficulties that he had endured because of his skin colour in the context of the wider struggles of black people in the continent of Africa.

The general British reaction to the book was mixed, but in the Cold War atmosphere of the 1950s, its contents inevitably led to Constantine being dubbed in some quarters as a communist agitator. It was an allegation he was prepared for; in the book itself he had complained that any black professional who 'associates himself with any progressive movement for his race … is almost certain to be labelled communist', and that 'the red stick is so convenient at the moment to beat a black back'.

Constantine certainly had a level of sympathy for communism, partly because of what he had read and heard about communist bloc attitudes to race; his friend Paul Robeson, who had received death threats as a result of his associations with the Soviet Union, educated his son in Russia, and other black friends had 'considerable personal, social or business contacts with that country'. This led Constantine to conclude that 'whether we like it or not, belief in class distinction stemming from birth or wealth has been eliminated in Russia, and with it has gone the feeling of natural superiority of white over black'. He also felt that the spread of communist ideas in colonial territories, especially in Africa, was an inevitable result of the desire for 'anything better than the torture of today'. He warned: 'It is no use shouting at the negro that democracy is better than communism. It may be better for you. It is not better for him. He only knows what democracy does to him when it makes him carry passes, shuts him in slums, pens him in land-sick reservations, half starves him and his wife and children.'

This did not mean, however, that he was in favour of what he referred to as the 'half religion' of communism; only that he understood its appeal to those with no hope. 'It is from ignorance under oppression that much political tragedy begins,' he argued. 'Unless democracy is somehow made to mean freedom to the enslaved and hungry coloured millions of Africa, then the whisper of communism will bring catastrophe for them and the whites alike.'

Colour Bar caused a stir in the national newspapers, which, on the whole, were reluctant to give it their stamp of approval. Lord Hemingford, reviewing the book in the *Daily Telegraph*, suggested it would come as an 'uncomfortable shock' to complacent readers, but added that it could also do 'infinite harm' to those who were not well versed in the history of colonialism and therefore would

Always in demand: signing autographs at Hemel Hempstead cricket week

not be able to 'separate the grain from the chaff'. Parts of the book were just not fair, he argued. 'Mr Constantine spoils his strong case not only by cluttering it up with trivialities but also by buttressing it with untruths.' The *Times* was rather more sympathetic, though still scathing. Constantine, it said, was 'an obviously likeable and sincere man' who, the book clearly showed, 'is suffering from an open wound' inflicted by racism. 'What he has to say should be read with humility and could have a useful effect on the public conscience,' it argued. But the author, alas, 'writes with less authority' on the colour problem around the world and his words on Africa are 'often erroneous and therefore most unfair to a well intentioned and hard worked British administration'.

Certainly *Colour Bar* brought Constantine into conflict with conservative elements of British society, and he claimed there were even attempts to thwart its publication. In a private letter dated 25 March 1961 to an Australian correspondent, Austin Jedick, who was looking at the possibility of producing a German translation of the book, Constantine said: 'The Catholics in Britain were some of the heaviest critics – they used all sorts of stratagems to frustrate extensive circulation [of *Colour Bar*], and more than that I believe influenced the non publication of a second edition. Because of this book I was dubbed a communist and this was spreading to such an extent that I felt something had to be done about it. One Sunday in Manchester I got on the platform and related what was being said, and I retaliated with these words: "I would rather lie in the gutter with white communists sharing their common lot than be given the exclusive right to the gutter because I am a black man." I asked the reporters to take note, but it never appeared in any of the English papers. I was, however, successful in quashing this propaganda, for at the time I knew nothing, and even to this day know less, about the philosophy of communism.'

Frank Birbalsingh, academic and writer on the Anglophone Caribbean, noted that throughout his writings and speeches, Constantine revealed 'frustration, sadness, disagreement certainly, but neither bitterness nor animosity' over the issue of racial discrimination. In *Colour Bar*, he came as close as he ever did to moving away from that measured approach. With the book out of his system and a new life beckoning in Trinidad, Constantine was able to turn his attention to how he could bring into action some of the plans he outlined in its pages; how he could contribute in a more concrete way to ushering in a bright new post-colonial dawn in his own country. In a 1954 farewell broadcast called 'Return to

Trinidad' (which an internal BBC memo described as 'outstanding to the point of being a landmark in Light Programme history'), he set out his hopes for the next passage in his life. 'I owe my country an effort,' he said. 'I owe something to them, coming back there and trying to teach them what I have learned; and perhaps learning myself a little bit of the progress they have made.'

6 Island politics

Late 1954 was a propitious time for Constantine to arrive back in Trinidad & Tobago. Change was in the air. The twin-island state was still firmly ruled by Britain, but since 1945 all its adult subjects had at least been granted the right to vote in elections to the Legislative Council of Trinidad & Tobago, which worked with the British-appointed Governor. While Constantine had been away in the 1930s, the British West Indies had been riven by serious civil unrest, militant trade union organization and growing political tension as ordinary people began to rise up against grinding poverty and white colonial rule. In Trinidad, the labour riots and strikes of 1937 brought turmoil to the country's oilfields that spread to the sugar factories, leading to the arrest and imprisonment of the trade union leader Uriah Butler. Across the Caribbean, the black nationalist teachings of thinkers such as Marcus Garvey gained widespread support. As a result, the British government set up the Moyne Commission in 1938 to investigate social and economic conditions in the British territories of the Caribbean. The findings of the Commission, which concluded that the disturbances could be linked directly to unemployment, poor education and health provision, low wages and unsatisfactory working conditions, persuaded the British government to usher in a series of social, economic and political reforms that would eventually open the door to independence for most of its territories in the region.

Constantine had not been wholly isolated from these developments: he was a regular winter visitor to the region during the 1930s, either for cricket or to spend time on holiday, and he was in contact with some of the leading thinkers in the region. His well stocked library included many books that touched on the future of the empire and showed his continuing interest in black nationalism. But he was on the periphery of the action, not yet an integral part of it. Now Constantine was pitching himself back into a country which at last appeared to see the possibility of taking control of its own destiny. Political discussion was on everyone's lips, and the West Indian cultural and nationalist renaissance that Constantine and CLR James had dreamed of in Nelson many years before was actually beginning to arrive.

If Constantine was not immediately clear as to what his role would be in this upsurge of activity, a few months of working in the country soon showed him his likely path. For the first few weeks after his arrival on the oil tanker *Regent Hawk*, his attention was given over to settling into his new home, a bungalow at 3 Immortelle Avenue, Pointe-à-Pierre, in the south of the country where he had worked so many years before. Norma had preceded him by a month or so to make preparations for Gloria's wedding in December 1954, which proved an emotional start to his homecoming. His early days were a social round of re-acquainting himself with old friends and official welcomes-home, including a civic reception in Port of Spain. His new job, which he began on 2 January 1955, was far more comfortable than anything he had known before in Trinidad. Because he had signed his contract in London, Constantine was on a favourable expatriate deal that allowed him an overseas break at the end of three years. His legal work was varied and interesting: examining the land rights for new oil exploration, preparing submissions on draft government legislation that affected the oil industry, overseeing contracts with third parties, advising on legal claims against the company, even, on one occasion, seeking redress for a senior manager over a defamatory newspaper article. He also began coaching young employees, as well as many of their children, at a local school. Although he was now into his fifties, Constantine also played cricket for the company on occasion, mainly on the Trinidad Leaseholds ground at Guaracara Park in Pointe-à-Pierre. Under his close supervision, the ground soon became a venue granted first class status, hosting touring international sides.

Constantine appreciated the privileges that his senior status at the company gave him, but although he could see that some progress had been made on the promotion of able black staff members, he was one of only a handful of black senior employees and found it difficult to feel fully integrated. Inevitably, then, the issue of race drew him back into activism. Initially he had assured Trinidad Leaseholds that he would stay out of politics while he was in the job, but that was easier said than done. Elections to the Legislative Council were due in 1956, and moves were afoot to create a new political party that would represent the mass of Trinidadians and their aspirations. There had been elections in 1950, but for fewer seats – 19 as opposed to 24 – and representation of the black and Indian masses had been fragmented among various idiosyncratic parties and a number of independents.

The new party called itself the People's National Movement, PNM for short, and its popular leader was Dr Eric Williams, a brilliant Trinidadian historian who had pursued an academic career as a professor at Howard University in the US and had recently lost, after disagreements with his employers, his job as deputy chairman of the Caribbean Commission. From his early years, Williams bore the burden of being the brightest student in Trinidad – and the expectation that he would pass the exclusive examination to become an 'Island Scholar', entitling him to study at Oxford University. As Clem Seecharan has pointed out in *Muscular Learning*, a study of cricket and education in the British West Indies, Williams's father, a black minor civil servant, 'like Lebrun Constantine, carried in him the fears and hopes that his son would achieve excellence in an area deemed central to colonial society'. The fortunes of both sons were eagerly monitored by the island's black population, which shared in their triumphs. Williams, ten years younger than Constantine, got his Island Scholarship in 1931, went to Oxford the following year, and achieved a doctorate – on the slave trade – in 1938. So the two were reaching impressive heights in their respective field more or less contemporaneously. While they were both ambitious and shared a pragmatic left of centre outlook on life, in character they were more different. Constantine was a fairly open book, but Williams was a much more complex man, charismatic in the public eye yet also introverted, gruff and uncommunicative. Constantine was free and easy with his friendships, while Williams opened up as a warm and caring person only to a small chosen circle of intimates, who could often find themselves suddenly out of favour for no obvious reason. Widowed in 1953, he eventually died (still in office as prime minister in 1981) as a lonely and reclusive man.

But when he launched the PNM he was very much the centre of attention.

On 21 June, 1955 – barely six months after Constantine had arrived in Trinidad – Williams established his political career in front of a large crowd at Port of Spain's central Woodford Square, a park facing the seat of the Legislative Council building, the Red House. Williams called for further constitutional and educational reform, wealth redistribution and a 'West Indian nationhood'. In a second meeting at the same venue in July, he announced his new party would be 'designed to offer the people of Trinidad and Tobago, whatever their race, class, colour or religion ... the key which they have not yet found and for which they are so desperately searching'. Constantine knew Williams reasonably well, as the younger man, while at Oxford, had spent some of his holidays staying with Constantine at Nelson, where he was fond of being taken to local pubs. Constantine also knew many of the men who now surrounded Williams politically – people such as the GP Patrick Solomon, Winston Mahabir, also a doctor but of East Indian extraction, and the lawyer Andrew Rose. He had come across them in Britain, where they had studied before returning to Trinidad. Constantine therefore felt relatively at ease with the key figures in this new movement; he was among people that he generally trusted. More to the point, however, he felt at home with the PNM's inclusive approach based around strong stances on anti-corruption, greater educational opportunity and nationalism.

Williams saw Constantine as an ideal person to have on his side, not just for his popular appeal but because he would broaden the political base of the party with his essentially moderate left-wing views. Constantine recognized Williams as a man to take Trinidad towards self-government. After some discussion with his boss at Trinidad Leaseholds, an understanding Scotsman by the name of JB Christian, Constantine was told that the company would not stand in his way if he wished to pursue his interest in the party. By 15 January 1956, when the PNM held its inaugural conference in Woodford Square, Constantine had been drawn so far into the web that he stood for the post of party chairman and was voted into office for a five-year period, with Eric Williams declared the party's 'Political Leader'. When the party was officially launched a week later on 24 January 1956, Constantine was already a founding member of its central executive.

His job as chairman was to set up the infrastructure of the party and to make the PNM the best organized party in the country – which he did. It was a gruelling task given the demands of his day job, and he spent the next several months in the run up to the general election burning the candle at both ends – waking, very often, at 4am to deal with PNM paperwork, then putting in a full day's work at Trinidad Leaseholds before attending party meetings in the evening.

Adrenalin kept him going, for these were among the most exciting times in Trinidad's history. The University of Woodford Square, as it rapidly came to be known, turned into a hotbed of political activity, where crowds of up to 25,000 people regularly gathered to listen to PNM speeches and lectures on subjects such as trade unionism, self-government, and the place of women in Caribbean society. There were 124 such lectures between 24 January and 20 June 1956 alone. The party set up its own newspaper, *PNM Weekly*, edited by Williams, with political thoughts and cricket reminiscences contributed, when he had time, by Constantine. The new party chairman travelled the country setting up regional party groups and building a national power base. He even led a team of 'PNM Internationals' (featuring politically sympathetic former West Indies players such as Victor Stollmeyer, Andy Ganteaume, and Puss Achong) in a fundraising cricket match versus The Rest on the Savannah in July 1956. Within a short time he was also preparing to stand for election as a member of the Legislative Council in the forthcoming general elections. Again JB Christian adopted a sympathetic line, though pointing out that of course he would have to resign from his job if elected.

The sudden turn of events had thrown Constantine into an overtly political atmosphere that he had shown little inclination to immerse himself in until now. He had once confessed to being 'afraid' of party politics – and had said that he 'never thought that the ability to bowl, bat and field could make me a desirable political commodity'. He was rather too much of a free spirit to sit comfortably in a political party. Yet he was the ideal figurehead for this new political movement – well respected, well known at home and abroad and, crucially for a party that was seeking broad support – a moderate who was not associated with any particular political dogma. That is not to say he had failed to take a keen interest in politics – far from it. His political views, however, were framed more in terms of racial politics than by social or economic concerns. He had met some of the leaders of Commonwealth countries and of Britain on his cricket travels, and was always careful to find out their views 'about improving conditions for coloured people'. He was unimpressed with Conservative prime minister Stanley Baldwin, who was 'evasive' on such matters, disappointed by Attlee, but found Herbert Vere Evatt, Australian Labour Party leader, 'forthright and tolerant'. He thought Nehru 'a great man indeed' with 'a first-class mind, keen and powerful

Before the thaw: Constantine, with daughter Gloria, in happier days with Eric Williams, who would later cut him adrift from Trinidadian politics

and sympathetic'; with a 'world wide understanding of coloured problems, not simply those affecting India'. He found Jomo Kenyatta, who he met on a visit to England, to be 'a peaceful man'. When he questioned the Irish president Eamon de Valera, he 'expressed strong views about liberty and equality for coloured people' and he knew Alexander Bustamante, chief minister of Jamaica and union leader, as well as his opponent Norman Manley, whom he judged 'a leader of great capacity and vision'.

PNM's programmes were a tidy fit for Constantine's racial focus, as everything the party was committed to would, almost by definition, uplift the conditions of black people. This was his chance to really make a difference. Political ambition for high office, as such, did not really come into it. Besides, whatever doubts he had about diving into the murky arena of politics were washed away by Norma. Without her support he would not have taken the plunge; but as usual whenever he stood on the threshold of an uncertain decision, she was there to give him a push through the door.

Constantine stood for election in the seat of Tunapuna, where CLR James was brought up, about six miles east of Port of Spain on the Eastern Main Road. It was a tough seat to win, as he would have to beat off a strong challenge from the Mayor of Port of Spain, S Mathura of the Peoples Democratic Party (PDP). In a country that had grown to 750,000 people, of whom around 47 per cent were of 'negro' origin, 35 per cent 'East Indian', and 14 per cent 'mixed', the PDP drew its support mainly from the Indian populace and from those in business, while the PNM – although it had Indian candidates – was mainly supported by the black working class. Constantine noted with interest that the Catholic church advised the electorate to vote against his party, mainly because it was in favour of birth control and state control of education.

As an indication of the great clamour that his candidature had aroused, Constantine was able to launch his personal election campaign in August 1956 before a crowd of 7,000 people. On election day, 24 September 1956, he won on a turnout of 87.4 per cent by a slender majority of 179, garnering 6,622 votes to Mathura's 6,443. As with his other PNM colleagues, he had largely won on the back of the black vote, but had also called on every ounce of his fame, goodwill and prestige to bring the seat home. His PNM colleagues were under no illusion that only Constantine (perhaps with the exception of Williams) could have delivered the constituency. As it was, it was still one of the closest contests of the election.

The result was also one of the highlights of a great day for the PNM, which won 13 of the 24 seats it contested in the election, making it the largest party in the Legislative Council ahead of the PDP on five, Trinidad Labour Party (2), The Butler Party (2) and two Independents. For the first time in its history, the black majority now exercised some semblance of power – and Constantine was in at the start. His election meant he had to resign from his Trinidad Leaseholds job, so he and Norma moved to a house on Tunapuna Road in Tunapuna at the heart of his new constituency.

Governor Sir Edward Beetham called on Williams, now chief minister, to form a government. At the first meeting of the Legislative Council on 26 October 1956, Williams gave Constantine the role of minister of communications, works and public utilities in an eight-strong cabinet. It was a key appointment, for the PNM desperately wanted to demonstrate that it could be a more efficient provider of infrastructure than the British. Constantine had responsibility for a budget that represented around half of all government spending at the time, and he roamed over areas such as the meteorological service, civil aviation, water, roads, licensing, postal services and the railways. He immediately began to oversee a five-year plan that began a number of road and bridge building projects, including the building of the Beetham Highway, saw some expansion of electricity services and water supplies, a school building programme and attempts to improve the tourist potential of Tobago. The first budget included plans for extended harbour facilities in San Fernando, a new terminal at Piarco airport, replacement of the ferry to Tobago, and a new fish market in Port of Spain. Much of this was to be provided by a substantial direct labour department that employed tens of thousands of people by 1960.

A large part of Constantine's brief was concerned with trying to bring Trinidad into a modern age that was clearly going to be dominated by the car. He steered the Motor Vehicles and Road Traffic Bill through Legislative Council in an attempt to regulate parking and set up one-way streets in built up areas. He was also keenly interested in how to reduce road traffic accidents, and devoted his first speech in the Legislative Council – on 16 November 1956 – to a disposition on street lighting and road safety – issues that he spent a fair deal of time contemplating. In his five years in office, more than five times as many miles of road were built than in the previous half a decade, and he supervised a significant programme of bridge building. But he also had important decisions to make on the future of Trinidad's ageing railways, and on what to do about the sea link between Trinidad and Tobago. Trinidad's 120 miles of steam railway were gradually becoming less used by the public and more uneconomical to run, with old rolling stock that would be costly to replace. A 1956 inquiry had recommended that the network should be closed down, and Constantine began to oversee a slow run down of the service. However, he executed something of a U-turn in 1960 by deciding that the railways should be given a stay of execution for at least another five years, buying some new stock in the process and effecting repairs to some old machinery. A typically pragmatic move, this was partly due to concerns about the availability of public transport in Trinidad, as Constantine's efforts to secure a decent bus network had been undermined by the failure of two private companies to deliver the necessary standards on route concessions he had awarded. As a result he took the system into public ownership, where he could exercise more control.

In such matters, Constantine generally progressed with calm reassurance, as he did in March 1957 when he moved, by most accounts, swiftly and efficiently to cut short a water crisis caused by piping problems in San Fernando. But the future of the Tobago boat service, to his irritation, proved to be rather more controversial and time consuming than he would have liked. The two passenger and cargo steamers, SS *Trinidad* and SS *Tobago*, which plied the seven-hour route from Port of Spain to Tobago's capital, Scarborough, had come to the end of their working lives. Constantine engineered what he believed was a neat stop-gap solution, selling the two un-seaworthy boats and arranging the long term charter of a larger ship – *The City of Port of Spain* – to avoid the cost of maintenance and repairs while new vessels were being built. To his chagrin, however, opposition members of the Legislative Council seized on the deal and intimated, using the cover of parliamentary privilege, that there was the whiff of corruption about it. Constantine was attacked in the December 1958 budget debate over accusations that the £8,000 he had been paid for the two condemned boats was well short of what could have been achieved. In the most high profile and intemperate parliamentary speech he ever made, Constantine erupted in indignation. 'I have travelled the five continents and I have been respected and looked upon as a man of integrity, a man that is honest, and I shall be loath to stand in this council and have members make insinuations and charges against me without registering a solid word of protest,' he said. 'I hope I may not be immodest when I say that many people never knew of the West Indies until they got to know of Constantine, and if this is the thanks I am going to get from the country for the service I have rendered abroad, then I hope I will live long enough to regret the day that I entered into politics.'

In many ways this was a defining moment for Constantine and his involvement on the political scene. As a man who took a moral stance on life, he was genuinely hurt and outraged that his integrity could be impugned on such a small evidence base – and angered that what he saw as a sensible solution to a difficult problem could be attacked purely for the purposes of party political point scoring. 'Many of us are the worse off for being in politics, but it is because we love our country and our people,' he told the council.

While Constantine's words may have said much about his sense of fair play, they did little for the perception of him in the public arena. It was far too touchy a response for a major politician, especially in a country known for its love of spicy repartee. Nor was it in the established calypso tradition of 'picong', in which calypsonians improvise savage on-stage put downs of their opponents, who are then expected to fire back the personal abuse with interest.

For the electorate, which already had some underlying misgivings about Constantine's absent years abroad, it did not read well to hear him complaining that he had made sacrifices to come back – nor did it look good to see him claiming so much credit for putting Trinidad and the West Indies on the map. While Constantine's work in Britain to promote understanding of the West Indies was valuable, it was by now of only marginal interest to people at home. His protestations portrayed him as rather high and mighty, overly concerned with his personal prestige. What passed for dignified black pride in Britain could easily translate into pomposity in his homeland. His PNM colleagues, perhaps more hardened to the cut and thrust of local politics, also privately thought him guilty of those failings, even if they respected his achievements at the ministry. They knew that the divided opposition needed to find common ground to attack, and that anything was fair game.

In short, the speech was a miscalculation. It emphasized that Constantine was still, in many ways, an outsider, and it showed that he was a thin skinned politician, overprotective of his reputation. It also betrayed the fact that while Constantine genuinely wanted to serve his country, he sometimes saw this too much in terms of what his status and experience could do for Trinidad. Some may have noted with a wry smile that before Constantine had sailed for Trinidad in 1956, he had said that he was coming back to try 'to teach them what I have learned'. His opponents, latching on to this rather condescending attitude, regularly caricatured Constantine as an 'Englishman'.

In Constantine's defence, he genuinely felt that Trinidadian politics should be conducted in a 'gentlemanly' way, and that the Legislative Council should not become 'a privileged forum for defamation of character' as he described it in another 1958 speech defending chief minister Williams. In this sense he was not just worried about his own reputation: he was concerned that the new breed of West Indian politicians, preparing themselves for self-government, should take their nations forward in a dignified manner, marking out boundaries of respect and common decency that would help to build, if not consensus politics then an orderly way forward where political debate was not characterized by violent or destabilizing disagreements. Given the later descent into tribal politics in Jamaica and British Guiana, he may have had a point.

Undoubtedly, though, there was a personal element to Constantine's dislike of rough and tumble politics. Feted in public throughout his adult life, Constantine had rarely been used to having his actions or motives questioned, and his personal preference – as he had demonstrated elsewhere – was to tackle opponents with diplomacy and dignity. When he did not get the same response back, it came as an unwelcome shock. Later, in a broadcast in December 1963, he admitted that the worst thing about his political interlude was 'the bitter personal attacks' he endured, particularly at Friday question time. 'The statements made against me and my integrity so appalled me that I began to dread those Fridays,' he admitted. 'The things said could never be challenged in a court of law because they were protected by privileges. Politics is certainly a hard game.' The Trinidadian journalist George John, who knew Constantine well through his reporting on politics at the time, saw that parliamentary knockabout just did not conform to his friend's mannered view of how one should behave. 'He was a very gentle man, a product of the old school of conduct, and he was appalled at the behaviour of members of parliament, their personal attacks, their rudeness in debate,' he said. 'He found his comparatively brief flirtation with Trinidad and Tobago politics particularly distressing.'

Constantine had a heavy workload as a minister, but it was relieved by the odd visit abroad, including his first official West

Indies tour as a minister shortly after Christmas in December 1956. In the autumn of 1959 he returned to Britain in a governmental capacity (carrying out some broadcasting work for the BBC while he was there) then travelled on to Australia, where he urged the government to drop its 'White Australia' immigration policy, which restricted non-white entrants to the country. In 1958 he accepted the job of providing comments for Radio Trinidad during West Indies Test matches against Pakistan at TT$30 a day – with the approval of cabinet colleagues. But in 1959, when he was offered a similar deal at TT$25 a day, he turned down the opportunity to allay any impression that he might be neglecting his ministerial work.

Back home in Trinidad, he attended the second West Indies Test against England at Port of Spain in January 1960, where he found himself at the centre of a crowd riot that erupted as the West Indies batting slumped and a controversial umpiring decision sent the Trinidadian, Charran Singh, back to the pavilion on his Test debut. During the disturbances Constantine had to use his fielding skills to catch a bottle that was heading for the watching Governor. *Wisden* blamed the riot, which led to play being suspended for the day, on too much drink, gambling and the very hot weather. But Constantine, in common with other nationalist politicians, linked it mainly to underlying frustration at the slow progress being made throughout the West Indies on true self-government. The West Indies cricket scene, dominated as it still was by the issue of the white captaincy, was a microcosm of the frustration felt by the populace at large.

Presciently, Constantine had warned in *Cricket Crackers* that 'there may be some rowdy Tests played in the West Indies in the next few years unless this colour bar business is brought into the open and wiped out of the game once and for all'. He added that 'neither the MCC nor the West Indies cricket authorities can continue indefinitely to disregard the easily aroused and violent feelings of thousands of West Indian workmen; cricket is their hashish; it is a drug in their poverty-stricken and toiling lives which may inflame them to follies big enough to hit the European headlines one day soon'.

That was back in 1949, and he had warned then that something 'must be done soon'. 'Cricket is the most obvious and apparent, some would say glaring, example of the black man being kept in his place, and that is the first thing that is going to be changed,' he promised.

The case for a black captain of the West Indies had been an abiding theme of Constantine's cricketing life, given added emphasis because, had there been no colour bar, he would have been a natural candidate to have held the job. In his early international days, Constantine had no problem with serving under the white captaincy of Austin, who was in the team on merit, was a good leader of men and, as James said, 'was the natural captain of West Indies as long as he chose to play'. But on the 1928 tour, Constantine was scathing abut the aloof and weak captaincy of the white Cambridge undergraduate Karl Nunes, arguing that 'whatever they taught him at Cambridge it could not have been our respective merits as parts of a team'. In 1933, when another white man, Jackie Grant, was at the helm, he felt it would have been wiser to 'find someone who had a deeper experience of West Indies players and possibilities' and in 1939 he argued that Grant's younger brother, Rolf, had been given the job 'despite obvious inexperience, on the grounds that a white leader was better than any black man and certainly not on any test of ability that I could see'. Relations between the two were strained throughout the tour. On one occasion during the 1939 visit, when Grant sustained an injury, Constantine was handed the captaincy for a solitary game against Lancashire, after which he was hauled over the coals by the West Indies board for holding out for a draw. An indignant Constantine felt he had captained well, successfully closing out the game when he saw that a win was impossible. To his disgust, he was replaced as skipper for the next game at Lord's by another white Cambridge man, the even more inexperienced John Cameron. 'I felt I had done my job, and had I been a white player, no doubt I would have led the game at Lord's also,' he said. After Constantine retired he admitted to 'a sigh or two' at not having been captain of something other than a single Dominions game.

By the late 1930s, George Headley as well as Constantine had also emerged as a credible black captain, but the West Indies Cricket Board of Control could not bring itself to contemplate such a move. Constantine was not overly impressed by Headley's nascent captaincy abilities – he found him 'sound and sensible' rather than inspirational – but after the war he argued that Headley was nonetheless 'head and shoulders' above the two white men, Jeff Stollmeyer and John Goddard, who were put in his place. He was particularly scathing about Goddard, as he had not played Test cricket before his appointment and had sprung onto the scene 'full-fledged from Jupiter's forehead as captain of his country'. The appointment of white captains, argued Constantine, had fostered 'an atmosphere of servitude' and not until a black skipper could emerge would West Indies be able to capture the spirit and independence they needed to really attack an England team, rather than treat them with deference.

By the time Constantine had left the international game, he had reached such a state of militancy on the issue that he appeared to favour the appointment of a black captain regardless of the merits of any white cricketers, putting him at odds with those, including James, who argued that the job should merely go to the best candidate irrespective of race. Only by the appointment of a black leader, Constantine felt, could the West Indies attain the psychological advantage that they required over other countries – to overthrow the prevailing idea, as Hilary Beckles characterized it, that 'contest with England was essentially a non-political event in which "cousins" exchanged mutual admiration'.

Constantine had kept his thoughts about the captaincy largely to himself while playing cricket, but in *Cricket in the Sun*, published after his retirement from the first class game, he argued that 'every coloured player who has ever turned out in an inter-colonial side has been conscious of it, and it rots the heart out of cricket and always will until it is changed'. He added: 'The time has come when I have become nationalist enough to plead openly, knowing what will be said of me, that all this nonsense should come to an end. Until players and captains are considered on their merits by a justice blind to their skins, the West Indies will never take a place in Test match cricket commensurate with the skill of individual West Indian exponents.'

Now in a position of political power in Trinidad, Constantine at least had a chance to influence events in a more concrete fashion. The West Indies Board of Control was an independent, white dominated organization not given to pandering to the whims of black politicians, but with the change in the balance of power in Trinidad and other West Indian states, it now had to begin to take some account of wider factors.

Constantine was therefore an influential early figure in the campaign for a black captain of the West Indies. But it was CLR James who made the biggest impact. After spending many years in the United States as a Trotskyist thinker, author and agitator, he had returned to Trinidad at the invitation of Eric Williams in 1958 after an even longer absence than Constantine. James, too, immersed himself in the nationalist struggle and, as editor of the PNM's new weekly newspaper, *The Nation*, led the campaign for the Barbadian Frank Worrell to be appointed the West Indies' first black cricket captain. Worrell was a great cricketer and a natural leader of men, nicknamed 'the cricketing Bolshevik'. In many ways he was a similar figure to Constantine – a conscious black man, dignified, diplomatic, but outspoken and passionate when necessary – who had the respect of the cricketing world and a spiritual commitment to the West Indies.

CLR James, Constantine and the PNM, with their allies around the West Indies, skillfully played on the captaincy issue as a focus for nationalists from all parts of the Anglophone Caribbean – recognizing, as James said, that the issue was 'a gift from heaven' for those who required a hook on which to hang their nationalist aspirations. The captaincy issue neatly encapsulated many of the nationalist issues in a way that even the most unpoliticized of people could discern. What's more, it touched on an aspect of British West Indian cultural life that vast numbers of people in the region were both knowledgeable and passionate about – a populist cause that could foster solidarity throughout the region in a way that politicians had not been able to on other issues.

The matter came to a head during the 1959/1960 England tour of the West Indies, with James's 'Alexander Must Go' campaign aimed at the white captain and wicketkeeper batsman Gerry

Alexander, whose inexperience only helped the crusade. As a result of the pressure the authorities cracked, and after some prevarication Worrell was eventually announced as the captain for the 1960/1 tour to Australia. As Manley argued, when nationalists were pushing for either Constantine or Headley to take the captaincy, 'the system was shaken and under repeated attack from below, but the structure was still intact'. By the time Worrell and his supporters were mounting their challenge, the system had already changed significantly and 'was close to being dismantled altogether'. With black figures such as Constantine now in ministerial roles, it was difficult to sustain a position under which the region's team was perpetually headed by a non-white captain.

To the delight of Constantine and many others, Worrell's captaincy was an immediate success. The cricket he encouraged was so adventurous and entertaining that when the West Indies team left for home at the end of the highly entertaining Australian tour, which included the famous tied Test match at Brisbane, half a million people lined the streets of Melbourne to give them a ticker tape farewell. It would have been interesting to have seen if Constantine could have engendered a similar transformation had he been offered the captaincy many years before.

As well as the captaincy issue, things were also moving fast on other nationalist fronts. In 1959 Britain had agreed to give Trinidad and Tobago internal self-government with Williams as prime minister, and Constantine had played a role in the gestation of a British backed 'nation' of West Indies states – the West Indies Federation. When a series of intractable differences and squabbles between the main states led to the final collapse of the fledgling federation in May 1962, Constantine played a prominent part in successful negotiations for Trinidad's independence at Marlborough House in London, where his familiar face helped smooth the creation of the separate state of Trinidad and Tobago on August 31, 1962. It was a crowning moment in Constantine's career. By this stage, however, he was no longer an elected PNM representative. With voting for a new 30-member House of Representatives due in December 1961, he had decided that the cut and thrust of party politics was not for him, and that he should return to his legal work in some capacity. PNM won the elections even more convincingly than it had in 1956, partly due to the record of solid and tangible achievement that Constantine had delivered on bread and butter issues such as schools and roads. With independence beckoning, Williams was able to offer his colleague the new post of Trinidad & Tobago High Commissioner in London. Constantine was a sensible choice for the job; even tempered, highly knowledgeable about Britain and its people, and a perfect bridge for the two countries.

Just as Constantine had been a pivotal figure in the birth of the West Indies as an international cricketing force, so he was in the thick of things at the birth of independence in the British West Indies. Again his importance was just as much iconic as it was in terms of actual achievement. He had brought goodwill and a certain glamour to a fledgling party; his charisma was a big draw for the public, and his fame and good humour knocked off the slightly remote edges of Williams's personality. Despite his elevated status as a barrister returned from England, the fact that Constantine was well known as a self-made, hero-status cricketer among all classes of Trinidadians helped to soften the view of the PNM as a party led by lawyers, teachers and doctors. He was good for the party both internally and externally.

Williams had chosen Constantine to carry out an unfussy, sound job both as party chairman and minister, two of the most senior

Reluctant politician: Constantine played a key role in negotiating Trinidad's independence, but was not emotionally suited to the rough and tumble of party politics

posts in the country – and he had proven to be a good choice. In politics Constantine was by nature a doer rather than a thinker, certainly less cerebral than colleagues such as James, not as gifted and tactically astute as Williams. He was never a great contributor of new ideas in cabinet, nor was he an especially political man in terms of theories. The *New Statesman* said he had a 'reputation for quiescence in cabinet' and that 'he confined any critical remarks to private conversations with Williams'. He did think long and hard about politics, but preferred to roll up his sleeves and see what he could do in practical terms to bring about the changes he desired. His spell as a minister was therefore a successful one, marked by a general level of efficiency and clear decision making that helped establish the important point that Trinidad was not just willing but ready for self-government. He mastered his brief well, was popular and well respected among his civil servants (a feature always of his relations with people he worked with), a good speaker on the hustings (though slightly less so in parliament), and able to show a maturity in debate that some other politicians failed to possess. As always, he brought compassion and understanding to his task, was a good motivator and maintained his sense of fun. In particular his experience of journalism meant he was accomplished at smoothing over a sometimes hostile local press that was suspicious of the new politicians in its midst. As Williams's de facto number two, he was also a good settler of internal party disputes and of clashes of personality, and he played an important role in raising funds for the PNM from abroad, especially Britain.

Despite these positives, however, Constantine was not born to politics. He wanted to serve the West Indies, but without the level of scrutiny that political life necessarily involved. He was too sensitive to criticism, and his formative years of public speaking and debate at English rotary clubs and church halls had not been good preparation for the more robust atmosphere of West Indies politics. He did not have the craft of some natural born politicians – indeed did not want to possess it. He was also older than many of his colleagues and had developed an anglicized mindset that sometimes put him at odds with the party.

A classic 'returnee', Constantine had re-discovered Trinidad as a small land with limited horizons – a place where his raised status could often become a source of distrust and where his experiences in the wider world were often discounted. He later admitted: 'I didn't see eye to eye with my countrymen on so many things. As far as they were concerned I had been abroad for 25 years living it up, while they had been suffering in conditions where the feeling of oppression was never far away.'

All of this meant that, after five years in government, it was a relatively easy decision for Constantine to change direction. That did not mean he was a failure in his short lived political career – far from it. He is still remembered fondly and with respect for the role he played in achieving independence. And that is not just with hindsight; when he left the country to become ambassador, he left it largely as popular as when he had arrived again in 1956. For a politician that was a considerable achievement.

7 Back to Britain

As the first Trinidad & Tobago High Commissioner in London, Constantine's brief from prime minister Williams was initially a fairly limited one: to help promote British investment and tourism in Trinidad & Tobago. But within a short time the post had developed into the classic ambassadorial job abroad: acting as the representative of the government, dealing with diplomats and looking after the welfare of Trinidad and Tobago citizens in Britain. Constantine himself saw the job as 'like being a public relations offer of the highest possible status', a salesman for his country, with the 'real burden' being that of 'fending for the interests of one's own countrymen in Britain'. This, he noted, was now especially important 'with so many more West Indians here now than there were ten years ago'.

The post of High Commissioner officially came into being on 14 June 1961 in a ceremony at Guildhall in London, before Trinidad had even gained full independence and while the West Indies Federation was still limping along. Constantine was a logical and popular choice for the job: many doors were still open to him, for he had only been away for six years. In a sign of his stature in Britain he became Sir Learie Constantine in the new years honours list of January 1962, only a few months on from his return. As the *New Statesman* noted, he still appeared 'a tall powerful man' despite his age, although he had a slight paunch and thick folds of skin on his forehead 'that give an appropriate elder statesman look to the athlete'.

Constantine's lively presence was always in demand at functions and gatherings, and his profile ensured that Trinidad & Tobago probably punched above its weight in diplomatic circles. He represented Trinidad & Tobago at an Independence Thanksgiving Service at Westminster Abbey in August 1962, had an audience with the Queen in November 1962, and was elected vice-president of the West India Committee, a long standing organization that deliberated on trade relations between Britain and the West Indies. A little more than a year into the job, in April 1963, he appeared on the highly popular *This is your life* TV programme, which chronicled his life with the help of surprise studio guests – an honour reserved for only the most well known of public figures and a sign that he had now passed firmly into the consciousness as a British treasure. The *This is your life* book, traditionally presented to the guest at the end of the programme, was inscribed with words honouring his 'sportsmanship, statesmanship and zest for life'.

A few days later Constantine received the freedom of the town of Nelson, at which Alderman John Shepherd recorded that Constantine's success was 'never won at the expense of honour, justice, integrity, nor by the sacrifice of a single principle'. In the same year he also appeared on BBC Radio's *Desert Island Discs* programme, another firm public favourite, choosing among the records he would take with him to a desert island "Old Man

River" sung by his friend Paul Robeson, "Softly Awakes My Heart" by Marian Anderson, and the calypso "Australia Versus West Indies" by Lord Beginner. Later, the National Portrait Gallery commissioned a bronze bust of Constantine by the sculptor Karin Jonzen. He also came to even further attention and acclaim as one of the central characters and heroes of James's classic and part-autobiographical *Beyond a Boundary*, published in 1963, which for the first time put West Indian cricket into its social, political and historical context. It told, among other things, the story of how Shannon Cricket Club and the Savannah matches helped reflect and shape the lives of ordinary Trinidadians. With large sections devoted to singing the praises of Constantine, the book also put the High Commissioner's name in front of a new generation of cricket fans who had not seen him play.

However, Constantine's high profile did not always gel with the discreet requirements of his new job, and it wasn't long before he found himself at the centre of some unwanted attention. Once again race was the issue. While Constantine had been away in Trinidad, Britain had seen the beginnings of a dramatic rise in West Indian immigration, largely due to a post-war labour shortage and the need to fill new jobs in public transport and the National Health Service. There were now around 115,000 West Indians in Britain, mainly in the poorer parts of urban areas such as London, Birmingham and Nottingham. A consequent rise in black/white tensions manifested itself in colour bars in housing and the workplace, as well as racial conflict on the streets, including the 1958 Notting Hill riots in London. The riots, which lasted for several days, largely took the form of white mob attacks on black people and their friends, and were a key event in British race relations, challenging the often complacent official line that all was generally well when it came to interaction between whites and blacks. For many observers, the disturbances for the first time gave substance to the arguments that Constantine had outlined in *Colour Bar*. Constantine felt acutely, as he always had done, that he should use his privileged position to speak out for, and help, those West Indians at the sharp end of such difficulties. As High Commissioner he took on a number of race-related cases, including, in January 1963, those of two West Indians – a barrister and a schoolteacher – who had wrongly been accused by the police of stealing a car. As well as being generally supportive to them, he arranged legal help for both, and when they were acquitted of the trumped up charges, advised them to bring a case for compensation for false imprisonment and malicious prosecution, resulting in damages of £8,000. His largely behind-the-scenes role in these kind of affairs was in tune with his diplomatic role, but his more interventionist stance on another racial issue drew some of his other tactics into question.

The source of the trouble was a dispute over racism at the Bristol Omnibus Company. In April 1963 the company had refused to even consider a job application from a Jamaican immigrant, Guy Bailey, for a conductor job on the buses in Bristol, stating that it had a ban on the employment of black labour. While racial discrimination in employment was still legal at the time, a young mixed race community worker, Paul Stephenson, took the story to the newspapers and in short time local activists, including the local MP Tony Benn, had begun to organize pickets and a bus boycott on the lines of civil rights protests in America. It was the first such racial action of its kind in Britain.

Constantine took great interest in the dispute for, like his Imperial Hotel case, it was just the sort of defining confrontation that could neatly crystallize the positions of the two factions on either side of the colour bar. It was also something he felt he could do something about, not just because of his High Commissioner status but because it was similar in nature to some of the disputes he had dealt with as Welfare Officer in Liverpool, and because he also had useful contacts with officials at the Transport and General Workers Union (TGWU), which was heavily involved in the situation. The opportunity for intervention presented itself fairly swiftly when Constantine made a weekend visit to watch the West Indies touring side play Gloucestershire at Bristol in early May.

Constantine had already written to the Bristol Omnibus Company, but while he was at the Bristol match he made a statement to the press criticizing the company's policy, pointing out that in the nearby town of Bath the same company did not impose such a ban. He also spoke about the matter on the BBC and had private talks with the Mayor of Bristol and with Frank Cousins of the TGWU, whom he had known from his welfare ministry days. At the end of the weekend he returned to London, where he then issued a statement saying he was pleased to see talks underway. Later he wrote an article for a Bristol paper on job discrimination in general but clearly using the incident as a hook on which to hang his views.

The intervention of such a high profile personality took the story on to a new level of importance, and was a significant boost for the campaign. Constantine's comments and influence undoubtedly helped to bring about a speedy resolution to the dispute, bringing pressure to bear on the Bristol Omnibus Company and the TGWU. Within a few weeks the company had begun to hire black drivers and conductors – and Constantine and Norma were pictured in the press with one of them, the Jamaican Norris Edwards. The boycott helped to challenge official complacency about racial injustice in Britain and was another contributory factor in the creation of the first Race Relations Act, which followed two years later with the advent of a Labour government. Tony Benn later revealed that the Bristol affair had finally helped to convince the Labour Party leader, Harold Wilson, of the need for such legislation.

Constantine was privately satisfied with the role he had played, but he was to pay a high public price for his intervention. Politicians in Britain and Trinidad were apparently not best pleased that a diplomat, however noble the cause, should make such a blatant political intervention in the internal affairs of a host country, especially given that the situation had not actually involved one of his fellow countrymen. The Bristol buses affair was strictly nothing to do with Constantine, and in diplomatic terms he would have done well to keep well away from it. He should also have consulted his government before acting in the way he did. He does not appear to have done so, preferring instead to act impulsively and on his own.

When news reached him that both Eric Williams and Duncan Sandys, the UK'Minister at the Commonwealth Relations Office, felt he had overstepped the mark, Constantine flew to Trinidad to seek a meeting with the Trinidadian Prime Minister. But Williams, apparently upset that Constantine had left his post in London without seeking permission, made himself unavailable. It is unclear whether they did see each other eventually, but there have been suggestions that some kind of meeting did take place, and that when it did, Williams decided only to listen, not to speak. Constantine, wounded and puzzled by the reaction, decided that his time was up. Having signed a fixed contract as High

Commissioner, he had only a few months left before renewal, and decided on his return to England to make it known that he would not be making himself available for a second term. Williams, who had by now begun to fall out with a number of his long valued political friends, including CLR James, appears to have made no attempt to reverse Constantine's decision. Although it is not entirely clear why the Prime Minister should have been so keen to abandon his long time friend and admirer – and at the time few details emerged of machinations behind the scenes – Williams's political career was marked by the serial dumping of people whom he had elevated to high office. His biographer Ken Boodhoo observed that 'as the years rolled by, person after person was used and discarded – sometimes even destroyed, if he could not be got rid of any other way'. Even Williams's daughter, Erica, admitted that her father had 'a propensity for putting people in cold storage for infractions both real and imagined'. Constantine was just one of that number. Some observers believed the Prime Minister wished for a lower profile High Commissioner and, feeling threatened or irritated by what must have felt like the near-adoration of Constantine in Britain, decided that he was no longer fit for purpose. The end of their previously good relationship was a matter of deep sadness for Constantine, and another reason for him to add to his distaste for politics. Williams, pointedly and perversely, made no mention of Constantine in any of his later memoirs.

Constantine said very little about the affair to anyone, even years later, and only occasionally opened up a little in private conversations with intimates. The journalist George John did, however, witness the extent of his feelings at first hand. 'I came to know about the breakdown in the relationship between the Prime Minister and the High Commissioner by odd circumstance,' he said. 'I was in London in 1963 and paid my usual courtesy call on the High Commissioner. He invited me to a lunch he was hosting at his home. At some point … Constantine was called away to the telephone. He came back with a grave face. He would be going to Port of Spain immediately and he did not know if he would return to London as High Commissioner. A year or so before Constantine died, I met him on upper Frederick Street in Port of Spain. He had been seeing his doctor. We chatted for a while on the subject of British honours for Trinidad and Tobago citizens, which he knew from reading [my articles], I was against. But there was no recrimination, only the old friendliness. On parting he said this to me, and I quote: "George, I want to tell you something. There is only one man in the world, if I was in a room and he walked in, I would walk out. That man is your Prime Minister." He spoke those words without any heat, any display of emotion, just matter of factly in his usual calm voice. Clearly, however, the hurt had run deep, had left scars and had forced him into a totally uncharacteristic attitude towards a fellow human being.'

Constantine's resignation was a curious affair, partly because his actions, in the general scheme of things, could hardly rank as a terrible misjudgement. He later claimed that in fact there was very little if any diplomatic fallout in Britain from his behaviour, and that Sandys, for one, had personally assured him that he had not made any complaints about his conduct. While Harold Macmillan's Conservative government of the time was hardly positioning itself at the cutting edge of race relations, Constantine's stance on the Bristol buses affair did not pitch him into direct conflict with ministers nor, in any serious way, even against general public opinion.

Nonetheless Constantine had made a miscalculation. As a diplomat he was unwise to have gone to Bristol at the height of the controversy, unwiser still to have adopted such a high profile position, or to make public statements and to write newspaper articles. Even if the injured party in the case had been a Trinidadian, it would have been more in keeping with his diplomatic role to work quietly behind the scenes for a remedy. He could still have done this even though the case involved a Jamaican, while perhaps prevailing on the Jamaican High Commissioner to take up the cudgels on behalf of his own countryman (in fact the Jamaican High Commission did make such representations). Instead, he had allowed himself to become the newsworthy centrepiece of the whole affair.

The man himself, however, appeared to have no qualms about his actions. He was satisfied that his intervention had helped resolve the issue by giving it higher prominence, and in any case he had long since believed that he had a personal duty to help all West Indians in Britain regardless of whether he was a Trinidadian government employee or not. Untrained and inexperienced in his post, he was not a career diplomat, and though he did possess many of the attributes of a good High Commissioner, he did not have the natural instincts of one. By this stage in his life Constantine considered himself a spokesman for the West Indian people, and he was prepared to be outspoken in that self-imposed role. In a broadcast in December 1963 he admitted that he had 'decided to raise the level of the negotiations because those immediately involved had adopted fixed positions and wouldn't budge'. He felt the ends justified the means: that he was 'specially suited' for the job of sorting out the Bristol dispute. Constantine had also taken the same combative approach over an announcement by the British government that it would accept a batch of (white) Maltese immigrants into the UK in the wake of the closure of a naval base in Malta, even though this would probably be in contravention of the Commonwealth Immigrants Act of 1962. Strictly that was no business of his either, but he could not keep quiet on what he saw as iniquitous treatment of immigrants based on their skin colour, and according to the *New Statesman* 'he spoke out vigorously against the Immigration Act even while High Commissioner'. Speaking much later about the Bristol buses affair (for he was coy about the actual reasons for his resignation for some time afterwards) he said: 'When a coloured man in London is getting his pants kicked, the people who kick his pants don't remember whether he is Jamaican or Trinidadian or St Lucian. It's a coloured man who's getting kicked, and so for my government to take the view that because he was a Jamaican I had no right to intervene, I could not accept'. In the Caribbean world, where the failure of the Federation had left each newly independent nation to fend for itself, that pan-West Indian stance was becoming increasingly old fashioned.

Later still, in a 1967 radio talk on the BBC with his old pal Rex Alston, Constantine conceded that there was validity to his government's view that 'I had exceeded my duties during the Bristol affair, that I should have recognized it as an internal matter for management and unions and refused to intervene'. But he maintained that he had no regrets about what he did, if only because it indirectly relieved him of the stifling diplomatic protocol of office which, he claimed, hampered rather than enhanced his aim of 'doing a job for my countrymen'.

As he had done sometimes in his private life, Constantine had occasionally, as High Commissioner, allowed the pressing personal problems of individuals to divert him from matters in hand. Howat claimed that 'any lame duck found him ready to listen' and that as a result he was 'careless with time and paperwork which was sometimes set aside in the interests of people'. He was also unwilling to delegate such cases to his staff. In short, there was too much of the welfare officer about him and not enough of the government focused diplomat.

Whatever his limitations as a High Commissioner, however, Constantine was once again a popular boss with his staff, always accessible, usually informal, showing the same general aptitude for careful organization that he had demonstrated as PNM chairman. He set up the office of the High Commission efficiently. But in the final analysis he was neither particularly successful nor especially unsuccessful as a High Commissioner. At the fag end of a political career, his experiences in the job taught him that he did not want to be in politics any longer.

Constantine worked out the last few months of his contract and took his leave of the job on 6 February 1964. There is no doubt that he felt hard done by and a little sorry for himself; when Queen Elizabeth and Prince Phillip sent him and Norma a signed photograph of themselves 'to remember us by' after his resignation, he reflected to one journalist: 'It's nice to know somebody liked us'. In reality, although he had been bruised by eight years of political activity, Constantine's general popularity in Britain was as strong as ever. This was to be reflected over the next few years in a plethora of honours and honorary roles in Britain that would establish him firmly as one of the 'great and the good'.

The ambassadorial existence at an end, Constantine and Norma moved from the commissioner's home at Grove End Road, just a stone's throw from Lord's cricket ground in St John's Wood, to an elegant third floor flat at 11 Kendal Court, Shoot Up Hill, in Brondesbury, north London, where he stayed for the remaining seven years of his life. Interviewed here in May 1964, surrounded by a large personal library of books he had collected over the years that reflected his long-standing personal interests in the Commonwealth, socialist and religious perspectives, race relations, Fabian politics, Catholicism, and even the Spanish Civil War, one newspaper reporter found a more reflective character than he had expected. 'Sir Learie, I feel, is a sadder and wiser man,' he said. 'Not a bitter man, just a profoundly disappointed and disillusioned one.'

Now aged 62, comfortably well off and with successful careers behind him as a cricketer, welfare officer, journalist, author, lawyer and politician, Constantine may have been excused for taking the opportunity to wind down. In some ways he did; from now on he would make his living through a patchwork of part-time and freelance posts that would dovetail with his interests in sport, race and small 'p' politics. But his services were still in demand in many directions, and the years that led up to his death were in some ways just as busy as those that had preceded them. While this involved him in a continuing round of social engagements – he was on the guest list to attend Westminster Abbey's 900th anniversary service in December 1965, and was a judge in the 1965 Miss World competition, for instance – he returned again to legal practice, sharing chambers in London with his long time acquaintance Sir Dingle Foot, whom he had met in the 1950s as a result of their mutual interest in the fate of South Africa. Foot, who had been both a Liberal and a Labour MP, shared many of Constantine's perspectives, including a pre-occupation with Africa and the Commonwealth. It was a late stage in life for Constantine to start practising at the bar, and realistically he was never going to establish himself as a top line barrister. The work he obtained was limited, but he was at least achieving a lifelong ambition by doing what he did. Despite his relative inexperience, he had been elected an Honorary Bencher of the Middle Temple in 1963, a form of recognition usually granted only to barristers of many more years standing. As so often, popularity with his peers had influenced the decision.

Constantine ventured twice more into book writing, producing, in 1964, *The Young Cricketer's Companion*, a coaching manual expounding the 'theory and practice of joyful cricket', followed two years later by *The Changing Face of Cricket*, a collection of thoughts on the modern game written with Denzil Batchelor. He also returned to broadcasting and journalism, writing on cricket in a column for Britain's oldest tabloid, the *Daily Sketch*, and, more lucratively, reacquainting himself with the BBC. Shortly after making his decision to leave the High Commissioner's job, Constantine had approached the corporation to see if there was any chance of work once he left, and he had made a broadcast entitled *No Stranger Here* on Christmas Eve 1963 while still in post at the High Commission, a well received programme in which he reflected on his years in England and the reception he had been granted.

He became a regular, if infrequent, broadcaster between 1964 and 1968, usually as a contributor to programmes on cricket, race relations and the Commonwealth. He was especially busy in 1965, taking part in at least 20 programmes made by the corporation. He also made his first step into the relatively new mass medium of television by helping with commentaries on some of the first televised one day cricket matches, a form of the game he had long favoured. In this way he again entered the consciousness of a new generation of cricket fans who had never seen him play. It would be wrong, however, to say that his television work was as successful as his radio presentations. For one thing his talkative style, perfect for radio, did not lend itself as well to the small screen, where there was a bigger premium on judicious silence. For another, his health was gradually beginning to fail, and breathing problems made it more difficult for him to talk well after climbing up the long ladders that led to the lofty commentary perches of the day. Nonetheless, he kept up his television work until 1969, two years before his death. His final radio broadcast, on a cricketing theme, was in 1970.

It was the BBC that also gave him his last appearance as a cricketer, when he played for the corporation's world service team, the Bushmen, in September 1964, against the village of Herongate in Essex. He had appeared for Nelson, who had now fallen on hard times, in a charity match during 1963 to raise funds for the club. And he was still playing the odd game of cricket in 1964 for the Cricket Writers XI, despite debilitating attacks of bronchitis. He kept in contact with the sport through honorary membership of various cricketing bodies, including the Forty Club, the Lord's Taverners, the Lancashire and Cheshire Cricket Society, and the Wombwell Cricket Lovers Society which, after his death, set up the Learie Constantine Memorial Award for the best fielder in the national 60 overs final. In 1960 he was among the first batch of non-white former players to be given honorary life membership of the MCC, a rare honour previously only offered to high ranking military officials or royalty.

In 1965 he was appointed by Harold Wilson's Labour government as one of the 15 council members of the new Sports Council, a national body set up to oversee and encourage sporting activity in Britain, as well as to advise government on how it should develop amateur sport and recreation. He also served on the council's coaching and development committee, travelling extensively around the country to help set up regional sports councils designed to act as a bridge between local authorities and local sporting bodies. Much of his work for the council involved speaking at conferences, appearing effectively as a goodwill ambassador. But he also took it upon himself to lobby for the availability of more public sporting facilities. For all this work he was paid £1000 a year.

The mid-1960s were a time of progress in Britain on race issues, and Constantine was to play his part in that movement. The Labour government's 1965 Race Relations Act, which for the first time made racial discrimination unlawful in public places (though not a criminal offence), set up a Race Relations Board to oversee implementation of the Act, investigate any possible breaches and suggest action and remedies in such cases. As the man behind the Imperial Hotel case, Constantine was a natural choice to serve on the new three-person board, and he was duly appointed as one of its first members in July 1967, under the chairmanship of the former Liberal MP Mark Bonham Carter.

By 1968, when a new Race Relations Act also made it illegal to refuse housing and employment to people because of their ethnic background, the powers of the Race Relations Board were extended and its size expanded to 12 members. Constantine remained in place, using his position to argue against the parallel Commonwealth Immigrants Act in the same year which aimed to supplement the Race Relations Act with a tightening up on Commonwealth immigration. Constantine's position at the centre of public debate around the Commonwealth Immigrants Act later spurred Jeremy Thorpe, the leader of the Liberal Party and a friend of Constantine's since before he was an MP, to suggest he would be a good candidate to contest the parliamentary Nelson and Colne seat, which became vacant as a result of the death of the long serving left wing Labour MP Sydney Silverman in February 1968. Thorpe felt that as a Liberal candidate Constantine could concentrate much of his campaigning on the Commonwealth Immigrants Act. But when the idea of standing was put to him, Constantine politely declined on several grounds: his age and increasing frailty, his dislike of party politics, and his respect for Silverman, with whom he had developed a friendship over his years as the MP for his 'home' town. He also appeared to feel that Nelson was a natural Labour constituency, and that he should not disturb that balance. In many ways his decision to forego the offer typified Constantine's fence-sitting on the cusp of Liberal and Labour politics.

He did, however, allow himself to become involved in other political projects. Constantine's continued interest in Commonwealth affairs since his return to England, as well as his impressive contacts list in Africa, had led him to become involved in attempts to quell conflict in the wake of a military coup in Nigeria in January 1966. When Sir Abubakar Tafawa Balewa, the first Prime Minister of independent Nigeria, was overthrown and kidnapped in the coup, Constantine was enlisted by the human rights charity Amnesty International to fly to Nigeria to try to seek his release. His fraught six-day sojourn in the country – the first time he had been to Africa – was largely a fruitless one. He discovered soon after his arrival that Balewa had already been assassinated. But Constantine's intervention on behalf of the regional political leader Chief Obafemi Awolowo, who had been imprisoned during the coup, met with more success. Although he was not able to visit him personally in jail, he managed to communicate with the chief, and while other factors played a larger part in Awolowo's eventual release from prison in the summer of 1966, Constantine had at least managed to register international concern. He produced a report for Amnesty on the overall situation in Nigeria.

Constantine's long association with the BBC also led to an invitation in 1964 to sit on the corporation's General Advisory Committee, and eventually, in July 1968, to the offer of a more powerful position as one of the 12 governors of the corporation appointed by the Prime Minister. A much sought after establishment role, the post also brought him £1000 a year over a five-year term, which went some way to providing a stable income base for his now more precarious finances, based as they were on a mixture of ad hoc legal work, broadcasting and writing. As a governor of the BBC his main role, with his colleagues, was to supervise the corporation's activities, to monitor its accountability to licence payers, and to help ensure that the BBC remained independent of political or commercial interference. This was a task that had become slightly more difficult in the mid-1960s as the BBC found itself under attack for allegedly showing left of centre bias.

The governors met every two weeks. Constantine was a valued member of the 12, partly thanks to his diplomatic skills as an interlocutor in internal disagreements. But his increasingly poor health meant his contribution to the cause was not as great as it could have been. The historian Professor Glanmor Williams, who was also a governor during Constantine's time, argued that he would have been able to make a much more telling contribution had he been appointed ten years earlier. 'By the time Learie joined the board he was already in broken health and this prevented him from making as great a contribution as he might otherwise have done,' he said. 'I have seen him there at times when his face was literally grey with strain and weakness, gasping desperately for breath and racked with bouts of the most painful coughing. Yet throughout it all he preserved the most resilient patience and good humour.' Lord Charles Hill, chairman of the BBC, took a similar view, admitting that 'the sad truth is that Learie came to us too late to play a really effective part. Already his chest had begun to give him trouble, with the result that his attendance was uneven and his contribution was inevitably marred by illness'.

The physical restrictions placed on Constantine by failing health must have proved a sore test for a man who was so fit during the earlier part of his life. It must have been doubly frustrating that just as he reached a position of real influence in Britain his body let him down. In the Queen's New Year Honours List of 1 January 1969 he was awarded a peerage – making him the first black man, though not the first non-white, to sit in the House of Lords (the Indian barrister and politician Satyendra Prasanna Sinha had become a peer in 1919). He claimed the honour as 'a recognition for all West Indians', and took the title of Baron Constantine of Maraval in Trinidad and Nelson in the County Palatine of Lancaster, acknowledging the two homes that were now so much a part of his being. There was considerable and exhausting media interest in his appointment, and, unusually, the ceremonial investiture at the House of Lords on 26 March 1969 attracted a full house, mainly as a result of his presence. More than 200 guests, including Barbara Castle, Michael Foot and Mary Wilson (wife of Harold Wilson) attended a reception hosted for him by Dingle Foot afterwards at which half of the invitees were West Indians.

Typically Constantine sat as a crossbencher in the Lords, preferring not to give his unqualified support to any one party.

Ennobled: Constantine at his investiture at the House of Lords in 1969, when he became Baron Constantine of Maraval and Nelson

But poor health prevented him from making his debut speech in the House until almost two years later. A plea for Britain not to allow its forthcoming membership of the European Community to eclipse its trade and cultural relations with the Commonwealth, the speech revealed his continuing concern that the post-colonial period should not lead to a wholesale ditching of the reciprocally beneficial links between Britain and its former empire. His concern to preserve what he saw as the best aspects of the Commonwealth increasingly fell on deaf ears, but the speech revealed in Constantine a consistently held view that, despite the considerable downside of colonial history there was much of value in the Commonwealth that ought to be preserved. Cricket, he believed, was a perfect expression of the appealing cultural mélange that the Commonwealth had created and which should not be sacrificed without great aforethought.

Unfortunately Constantine was not able to expand upon those or other views in the House of Lords, as it was the only occasion on which he was fit enough to speak. There is some evidence to suggest that he had actually been in line for a peerage in 1964, but that the move was blocked by Eric Williams when the British government sought his approval. If this was the case, then Williams did both Constantine and the House of Lords a grave disservice.

The sad reality of his last years, as Constantine's elevation to the peerage showed, was that his post ambassadorial rise to a position of stature and influence in Britain had been accompanied by a sharp fall in his ability to do anything of real significance in those roles. Perhaps the starkest evidence of this was his election to serve as Rector of St Andrew's University in Scotland, a prestigious post held in the past by the likes of John Stuart Mill, Rudyard Kipling and Field Marshal Sir Douglas Haig. Constantine had been invited to stand for election on 12 November 1967, and despite coming up against three strong candidates with Scottish connections – the Liberal Orkney and Shetland MP Joseph Grimond, the Scottish actor Sean Connery, and the Scottish music director and conductor Sir Alexander Gibson – he won by a substantial majority of student votes. In a sign of things to come, Constantine was not present for the vote, as he was recuperating in the Bahamas after having had an operation in London. But he made his first significant intervention in the university's affairs shortly afterwards, when he publicly protested against what he called St Andrew's 'deplorable' plans to stage a rugby match against a touring whites-only rugby side from South Africa's Orange Free State University. Although St Andrew's went ahead with the fixture anyway, the controversy generated by Constantine's intervention fed into the fevered debate about British sporting relations with South Africa, which erupted later that year in the shape of the D'Oliveira affair, over the initial non-selection of the black cricketer Basil D'Oliveira for an England tour to South Africa. Constantine took a public role in condemning that decision too, and when a U-turn over D'Oliveira's selection led the South African government to refuse to play an England team in which he was picked, the country was expelled from international cricket until the fall of apartheid in 1994. Back in 1959, when the West Indies board had come up with the idea of sending an unofficial 'goodwill' team to South Africa, Constantine had opposed the plan, even though Frank Worrell would have been captain and the eight matches on tour would all have been against black and 'coloured' teams. In the end the tour did not happen, but Constantine had adopted a more radical position on the matter than either CLR James or Worrell, who were both prepared to see it happen.

Constantine was officially installed as Rector of St Andrew's on 17 April 1968, receiving an honorary degree as doctor of law in the process and choosing 'race in the world' as the topic for his grand acceptance speech. This was a largely ceremonial setting where it would have been a lot easier to talk about something less controversial. But Constantine never shied away from the uncomfortable, and when he spoke about the subject to largely white audiences he could in any case be relied upon to broach the topic with humour as well as tact. Besides, he knew that he had been elected to the rectorship precisely because he was black. 'You have by the election of a coloured man to be your rector served notice on the world that you have broken down the barriers and removed the obstacles standing in the way of progress,' he told his audience.

His speech was a promising start to his duties, but thanks to a mixture of poor health and other commitments Constantine was never able to build upon it. The rector was not expected to spend large amounts of time in his role; indeed the university, mindful of Constantine's health problems, had given him the luxury of choosing an 'assessor' to be his representative for much of the time. But his continued absence from university affairs soon turned some undergraduates against him. By 15 October 1969 the St Andrew's student magazine, *Aien*, while acknowledging that Constantine was by now severely debilitated with chronic bronchitis and sometimes hardly able to walk unaided, was nonetheless complaining that he had shown little inclination to become involved with the university even in his earlier, marginally fitter days. 'Many students have been dissatisfied with Constantine's performance as rector throughout his term of office,' it reported, suggesting that he had shown a 'lack of interest' in the post throughout.

While Constantine appeared to have been influential in helping to raise money to build a new annexe to the university, *Aien* said he had been 'utterly useless' when it came to his responsibilities towards the students, chairing only one meeting of the university court, where he was supposed to represent student views. It accused him of being a 'bad rector' who had clung to the title even though he was 'incapable of shouldering the responsibility connected with it'. It recommended he 'should resign now of his own accord'. That month a meeting of St Andrew's students voted by 151 to 100 to ask him to step down, but the move was blocked by the Students Representative Council, perhaps because of the embarrassment it would have caused. Such a de-frocking would have been an unprecedented action, and given Constantine's state of health, it would have been a rather unfeeling one, even if the students had grounds for complaint. Constantine could, and perhaps should, have resigned, but he remained in post until his three-year term expired in 1970.

It would be wrong to dwell on the St Andrew's rectorship for too long, if only because it appears to have been the only honorary or public service role in which Constantine could justifiably have been accused of failing to deliver a valued contribution. It was one of the few times in his life when he did not live up to his oft preached mantra, drilled into him by his father, that 'if you're going to do something, do it properly'. However, his problems at St Andrew's were indicative of the growing difficulties that faced Constantine in the last few years of his life – not just in terms of his ill health and a slowing down of his natural vigour, but the growing perception that he was now part of a slow moving and self-satisfied establishment. While the criticism he received in this vein was probably a natural backlash against the plethora of honours and sinecures he received in his later years, it was also a function of the radicalized late 1960s and early 1970s, when reverence for titles and institutions was fast diminishing. As far as Constantine was concerned, his elevation to the House of Lords, the Race Relations Board and a BBC governorship was evidence that he had been able to make progress not just on his own behalf but for the black people he saw himself as representing. But for many of a more radical or cynical disposition it was merely proof that he had become a poodle of the establishment, a token dark presence in its ranks. The influential satirical magazine *Private Eye*, founded in 1961, had taken to lampooning Constantine as an ineffective, de-racinated character, and Constantine himself was aware of similar caricatures of himself in other spheres, not least among the post-war West Indian immigrant community, which was generally of a different generation to him. Writing privately to his cousin Hubert Andrews in later life, he suggested that 'many of my countrymen would be jealous and critical, feeling as they do that I am a black-white man'. His papers also show evidence that he was personally confronted with the view that he had become an 'Uncle Tom' figure. An anonymous 1970 letter, which he kept, accused him of 'degenerating into becoming a showbiz tool of Powellites', although it is not clear how or why supporters of Enoch Powell, architect of the infamous anti-immigration 'Rivers of Blood' speech in 1968, could make use of him. Constantine was disappointed and upset that he should be viewed in such a way, even if only by a minority. There may have been an inkling of truth in the generalized portrayal of him as self-obsessed and self important. As a self made man, Constantine certainly enjoyed the status that the various appointments and honours gave him, even if he was always dismissive of being referred to as 'Sir' or

'Lord'. He was hardly now on the cutting edge of racial politics, which was increasingly influenced by notions of the black power movement. Financially he was relatively well off and his ermined life of engagements, cricketing dinners, functions and committee meetings had little to do with the experiences of the new West Indian immigrants. He was not of the same age as most of them, and had encountered his share of racism and hard times in a different era. This meant he did not share exactly the same outlook as they did. But to accuse Constantine of being a man neutered by honour would be to miss the importance of his role in post-war British life. By the time he had reached his mid to late sixties he was indisputably a representative man. If this laid him open to accusations of being a token black in white society, then a token he was, for he believed that the British needed to see, and to have, black people in positions of influence. His name in the frame was a start. Sam Morris, writing in the early 1970s, argued that his friend's presence and beliefs 'made him a symbol to a number of influential persons in this country who otherwise would not have given any thought to black potential', and that when confronted with allegations of tokenism, 'how right he was when he answered, in private conversation, that if there is one token this opens the way for another and another, and an accumulation of tokens could be very important indeed'.

Constantine would have seen little purpose in refusing the honours that came his way when he had always argued that such posts should be as available to black people as to white. Daughter Gloria, who herself rose to a prominent position in Trinidad as head of St Francois Girls College and later as an educational adviser to the government, said after his death that he felt it was his duty to be first in many things. 'He felt that if he'd messed up there wouldn't have been any others to come,' she argued. It was logical that Constantine should be the first black man in so many positions, for in truth there were precious few other prominent black candidates for such jobs. Constantine's sporting, political, diplomatic and public service background made him the ideal man to fill many of the posts he was given. He was also, crucially, well known and respected by the white population. The author Undine Guiseppe relates a story told to her by a Trinidadian parliamentarian who, in Constantine's later days, arranged to meet Constantine for lunch at a London hotel. When the hotel staff found out that Constantine was there, 'there was an almost total interruption in the ordinary routine of the hotel, as practically the entire staff endeavoured to obtain a glimpse of the great man or to pay him their respects'. George John also told of an experience in London in 1961 when, at a lunch hosted by Eric Williams and attended by British cabinet ministers and members of the Caribbean political establishment, Constantine was received by the British dignitaries 'with a display of affection and friendship that staggered the West Indians in that lunch hall'.

This was the role that Constantine played – of the respected black man in Britain. Many years later that may seem to have been a limited function, but in the context of the times it was an important one. Constantine was not there, in his eyes, to necessarily shake things up, but to be there, full stop. He would make as telling a contribution as he could while in office, but in all his appointments he felt the extra dimension of being black. Other prominent black figures who followed may have made more of an impact in terms of their overall contribution to public policy, but Constantine was the man who paved the way for them to do so. As Calder has said, the value in Constantine's progress lay in the fact that he was 'a token of the new status officially accorded to black people at the heart of the former empire'. To get where he did was 'a remarkable finale to the life of the son of a cocoa plantation foreman descended from slaves'.

Constantine's achievement, therefore, was more in terms of getting to the positions that he did than in what he did while he was in them. That said, it would be reckless to ignore the effect of his health on Constantine's ability to deliver once he had joined the ranks of the BBC and the Lords. He was a pensioner by the time he became a BBC governor and a peer. With better health he might have gone on to do more than merely hold such offices; he may have made a much wider impact that would have added to his legacy.

As a result of ill health, then, Constantine's last few years were essentially ones of valediction rather than achievement. Throughout the 1960s, in the damp British climate, he suffered with gradually worsening chest complaints and bronchial trouble allied to, of all things for a cricketer, lifelong hay fever and a late-diagnosed allergy to grass. By the summer of 1969 he was suffering serious bronchial catarrh and Norma's health was deteriorating too, though she hid it well from family and friends. The couple had spent three months on holiday in the warmth of Trinidad in 1968 and Constantine, on the advice of doctors, had been told to make a permanent move back to the West Indies. With their daughter and their grandchild Maurice now in Trinidad, it was a sensible final journey to make. Yet the work, and the allure of life in England, kept them there.

Constantine had long since acquired the 'dual identity' of many immigrants, finding that while he still nurtured deep longings to go 'back home' and 'to sit in the sun and tell stories of cricket', he also

Loving couple: Norma was the classic strong woman behind the successful man

felt that he belonged in England as much as Trinidad. He had now lived as long there as in his homeland; he had divided loyalties. And as Dingle Foot said: 'Although his heart was in Trinidad his great fame in public life was in Britain.' Paradoxically, the ill health that dogged the last few years of his life, while it necessitated his move back to Trinidad, probably also created an inertia that made him less inclined to leave. By June 1971, however, he had decided for sure (and announced to the Press Association) that he would be going back for his health. His doctors had told him that another winter in England would kill him, and plans for a once-and-for-all return were made. But he had delayed the decision too long. On

1 July 1971, at his home in London, at the age of 69, Constantine died peacefully in his sleep of a heart attack, perhaps due to the effects of bronchitis. According to his family, he had awoken in the morning, spoken to Norma for a while, and had gone back to bed. He never awoke again.

Despite his long run of bad health, no one had expected such an abrupt end. The family was in shock; Norma inconsolable. A state funeral was announced in Trinidad, and Gloria and her husband travelled to England to help with arrangements. On 6 July Constantine's body was flown to Piarco airport near Port of Spain, where the coffin was draped in the national flag by troops from the Trinidad and Tobago regiment and taken to lie in state at the Cathedral of the Immaculate Conception in the capital's Independence Square. Thousands filed past the coffin to pay their respects.

The grand 30-minute funeral service took place two days later on 8 July 1971, and was led by Archbishop Anthony Pantin, who described Constantine as 'a man who walked with kings without losing the common touch' – 'a real gentleman whose great achievements in more than one field were never allowed to go to his head – who remained a humble and approachable man'. In the front pew of the cathedral sat Eric Williams. Not far away was Clifford Roach, the Test cricketer. Lady Constantine sat sobbing throughout the ceremony.

As the coffin was carried out of the cathedral to the sound of the national anthem and a 19-gun salute, thousands of spectators lined the 10-mile route from Port of Spain to the village of Arouca, where Constantine was to be buried in the family plot at the local Catholic cemetery. Although this was a private ceremony with only close friends and family allowed among the graves, hundreds were packed outside to pay their respects, with a dozen or so hanging perilously from an overlooking mango tree. In a moment of unintended levity there was a loud crack just as the prayers were begun, and spectators looked up to see a man clinging on to a straining branch for dear life. As the prayers came to an end and the first volley of rifle fire echoed through the village, there was another louder crack, and the tree climber plunged to the ground with the broken bow, much to the barely suppressed amusement of the onlookers. Despite the solemnity of the occasion it was a moment that Constantine would probably have appreciated.

After the funeral, Constantine was posthumously awarded the Trinity Cross, Trinidad's highest honour, which was received by Gloria on his behalf. Later on 23 July 1971, in London, the British held their own memorial service for him at Westminster Abbey, with music by Bach and readings from the bible and John Bunyan – an accolade as high as any he had received in life. The main address was given by Dingle Foot and the second lesson by Harold Wilson, now leader of the opposition, with the ceremony broadcast partly on the BBC. An extraordinary number of tributes had poured in from around the world. He was greatly missed by many who had encountered his warm-hearted spirit, his love of life and his compassionate zeal. But none felt the loss more than Norma, the classic strong woman behind the successful man. Their enduring, loving, married relationship of 44 years had kept them both going against the odds on many occasions, and though the quieter of the two on the surface, Norma had so often driven Constantine along when his instinct would have told him to call it a day. Unusually for the times, Constantine would take Norma with him whenever he could on cricketing or business trips, and though firmly recognized as a 'man's man' he would return home from functions as soon as decently possible so as to be with his wife. In *Cricket in the Sun*, he described her as 'comrade, adviser and inspiration, summer and winter alike'. She had neglected her own health to look after his.

Now that he was no longer around, it was Norma's time to call it a day. After the funeral she remained in Trinidad with Gloria and her family, but outlasted her husband by just two months. She died, in her native land, on 4 September 1971.

8 Compassionate radical

Any assessment of the impact of Constantine's life must start with his years as a cricketer, for these were the basis of all that was to follow. If he had not achieved excellence in cricket, then the likelihood is that Constantine would have lived the life of quiet struggle that was ordained for him by Trinidad's colour-conscious outlook. Cricket gave Constantine more than just a leg-up to his later life of influence, however. It allowed him to make a significant contribution to West Indian society.

Constantine was, and is, an incontrovertible 'great' of the game. He achieved this status not by weight of runs and wickets, nor even by his superb fielding, but by his influence, his impact, his overwhelming popularity and the nature of the way he played the game. More than this, he helped define a specifically West Indian mode of play that was to become associated with the team for the foreseeable future – and which formed the foundation stone of the great West Indies sides of the 1980s. Neville Cardus, quite rightly, called him the 'spiritual father' of all the great West Indian cricketers who came after him. By helping to establish this identity in his own image, Constantine finally propelled West Indian cricket into the hands of the black majority. By doing so, he took it away from the more measured, anglicized approach of the colonial whites who had ruled it thus far. He did not engineer an overnight explosion, for West Indies cricket did not achieve the freedom it needed until Frank Worrell became its first black captain 15 years after the Second World War. But Constantine lit the fuse and continued to blow on it, even when he was out of the game. Given the societal and political importance of cricket to the inhabitants of so many British West Indian territories – plus the explicit links that were later drawn between cricket and the political struggle for self-government – it is fair to say that Constantine's cricketing feats between the wars sowed seeds for political change in the region. Although he was studiously non-political in public during his cricketing career, his actions on the field had their own politics about them – just as the play of his club, Shannon, also did. Constantine set West Indies cricket free.

Outside of the West Indies, however, he also made his mark as the finest league cricketer of all time, fashioning, in a comparable way, a crowd-pleasing template for league professionals and, through his sheer enthusiasm and skill, ushering in the golden years of league cricket in England. By establishing himself as one of the best paid and most popular of all cricketers based in the country, he also did much to dent the credibility of the class-ridden, amateur-dominated English first class game, which he helped to undermine in much the same way he helped to undercut the white, class-ridden and amateur-dominated West Indies hierarchy. He was by no means the only cricketer to engage in this battle, but he was one of the most influential.

After top-level cricket, Constantine could easily have faded into relative obscurity by returning to Trinidad or following a low-key career in law. But his decision to stay in Britain, partly fuelled by a genuine desire to serve those who were less well-off than himself, gave him a sense of direction that continued for the rest of his life. In many ways the war-time Welfare Officer job he took in Liverpool was the non-cricketing post to which he was most suited. It drew on many of his strengths – compassion, diplomacy, humour, organizational skills – and allowed him, for the first time, to deal directly with issues of race that had been uppermost in his mind for many years. He always felt more comfortable dealing with the social, rather than the political, fallout of race discrimination, and he delivered a valuable service not just to West Indian immigrants during the war period, but to the British government. His determination while in the Welfare Officer job to bring the Imperial Hotel legal case produced a high profile victory that set Britain on the road to the Race Relations Act, and if he had continued down the welfare track, Constantine's contribution to improving the lot of immigrants in Britain may have been judged as more significant and long lasting by some parties. It would not, however, have given him the prominent voice on race issues that his subsequent post-war broadcasting and writing career delivered. It would be naïve to think that the need to secure a decent income, his attraction to journalism and his desire to continue the connection with cricket were not important considerations for Constantine when he moved into print and radio, but it is clear that he also felt the media would give him the chance to get a message across. He was an accomplished and popular radio broadcaster, a decent journalist and an engaging author. But, crucially, all three avenues allowed him to venture into and express opinions on racial politics. As a broadcaster this was mainly in the form of reminiscences on his earlier life that successfully drew listeners into greater understanding of the nature of the West Indies and of the personal hurt caused by prejudice. With a few exceptions, his journalistic writing concentrated mainly on cricket, but his books, though also mainly cricket-focused, broke new ground for such a public figure, bringing discussion of politics and race into the cricketing arena long before the arrival of *Beyond a Boundary*. If the mention of racial matters was limited in scope in his early books, *Colour Bar* was a courageous volume that tackled racism head on, for a white audience, in common sense terms. While it was rough at the edges and never destined to stand in the pantheon of great works on the subject, it was an important contribution to the debate on prejudice in Britain, written by someone who had come to be considered as a trusted insider. Constantine's great strength on racial issues was that he was able to appeal directly to ordinary white Britons. He was allowed into their living rooms in a way that no other black person, certainly not remote intellectuals such as CLR James, would have been permitted. This did not mean his message was universally accepted, just that it was heard. His friend Denzil Batchelor, who often collaborated with him on projects in journalism and broadcasting, stated that Constantine was 'the only negro that I know who makes it impossible for you to forget that he *is* a negro – and who makes you wish you were fine enough to be a negro too.'

As a barrister, Constantine's impact was far less noticeable. In essence his career in law was a selfish undertaking with few wider impacts, though one of the driving forces behind it was to break free of the discrimination that he felt had prevented him from seriously considering a legal career back in Trinidad. After his qualification, his legal job at Trinidad Leaseholds and his small practice in London were decidedly low key. His impact on the profession was minimal. As ever, though, his presence in an area of life where there were few black faces helped to break down racial barriers.

Constantine's legal job did at least allow him an entry back into Trinidad, which in turn provided him with a platform to launch a political interlude that encompassed self-government and independence. Here his contribution was far more significant. His presence as a respected, moderate figure who appealed to the masses was one of the reasons that the PNM was able to garner as much support as it did – and so quickly. His organizational skills as party chairman delivered a strong regional base for the party and he was often the glue that held the PNM together in its early days. He also delivered a parliamentary seat that would probably have gone to the opposition if he had not been sitting, and as a senior cabinet minister presided over a lengthy period of solid achievement on transport and infrastructure that proved to the Trinidadian people and the British government that PNM could rule. In short, Constantine was a lynchpin in the Trinidadian journey to self-government, one of the key figures in West Indian politics of the 1950s. He was not a politician's politician, nor was he a natural to the game. At times he amused and bemused his fellow politicians with his over-sensitivity and his 'Englishness', his feeling that things could often be done better the British way. For much of his time both as minister and High Commissioner he felt himself an outsider and was frustrated by the insular attitudes of some of his colleagues. As High Commissioner, he lost his job partly because his pan-West Indian view did not chime with that of the politicians back home. But as a politician he discharged his duty, and for the most part, he discharged it well. It is, of course, impossible to assess how the course of events in Trinidad would have moved without him, but the likelihood is that they would have progressed less smoothly. Just as he was Eric Williams's trusted right hand man, at least until their fall out, he was also Trinidad's right hand man – a solid, dependable presence who helped steer the country to independence without histrionics. It was a personal release for Constantine to move out of politics, and it was probably just as well that he left when he did. The decade after independence was characterized by a strong growth in the black power movement in the West Indies and a move to more radical, confrontational politics. Constantine would probably have been a key target for the activists who pushed that movement forward.

After politics, in the decade of lofty public office that followed, Constantine sometimes found himself less able to deliver practical results than he would have liked. Although he continued as an influential broadcaster and built up an impressive portfolio of part time responsibilities, including his important roles with the Sports Council, the Race Relations Board and the BBC, there was a sense that his days of concrete achievement were drawing to an end. Largely this was due to failing health, but also because the roles he fulfilled were less visible, that he had necessarily become a committee man. His peerage theoretically gave him free rein to roam about the issues that were close to his heart, and he may well have been an effective, high profile member of the House of Lords. But that opportunity came too late. In the end, his chief importance in the last years of his life was as a respected black figurehead; a non-white presence in Britain's establishment. Arguments can be had about precisely how significant that presence was, whether it really made any difference to the lives of ordinary black people in Britain. But certainly many black people in Britain saw him as one of their champions. He saw himself in that role too, and spoke out frequently when he could easily have kept quiet. He wrote *Colour Bar*, defended Seretse Kharma, propped up the League of Coloured Peoples, took the Imperial Hotel to court, intervened decisively in the Bristol buses dispute, fought racism as a key member of the Race Relations Board, campaigned tirelessly on the black captaincy issue in the West Indies, helped to wrest the West Indies from British colonial control. More than that, he personally helped countless numbers of black people who came to him for assistance. That is not the record of a man who accepted the status quo, nor of a man who was happy to make compromises. Constantine may not have been a militant, but he was assuredly no conservative. *Wisden* probably had it about right when it called him a 'compassionate radical'. Constantine's dislike of party politics may have restricted what he could do on matters of race. If he had accepted one of the two offers he received to stand as a British MP, then maybe he could have achieved more on that front. On the other hand, he may have become more of a talker and less of a do-er – and the latter was his preference.

To some extent, Constantine's importance to the black British experience in the 20th century has been underplayed because of the kind of man he was. Though he was prepared to be controversial, he was not, at heart, a controversialist. He was an easy going man who could always be relied upon to reduce a perceived threat with some carefully worded charm or self deprecation. In essence he preferred to work quietly in the background on the issues that concerned him, trying to use his powers of persuasion on those he came into contact with. He could deal well with people of conservative views even though he did not share their politics, partly because his thoughts on the continued value of the Commonwealth gave him common ground on which to talk to them, partly because he was not cynical about tradition or moral values. Above all he felt he could show by dignified, friendly and personal example that black people deserved an equal place in British society. For many white people that is exactly what he did. His desire that West Indian immigrants should 'give variety and warmth and humour' to Britain and to 'do a jolly good job of work as well' was a picture of the immigrant, built largely in his own image, that did not resonate with some members of the increasingly radicalized younger generation of West Indians in Britain. But it was more in sympathy with the views of many white Britons. Constantine spoke to the white majority more than he did the black minority; deliberately so, for he believed this was how significant attitudinal change could be brought about. He asked for tolerance and respect; stressed responsibilities as much as rights, played a role that best suited his temperament. John Arlott argued that this meant 'he sustained his own position, and that of all coloured people, with a dignity and an absence of rancour rarely equalled by his reactionary opponents'. In doing so, he began to bridge the divide between the black Caribbean and white Britain.

Constantine may not have fully explored all the possibilities that lay open to him in his life, but he did lay the ground for others to follow. In many ways his heir was the slightly younger David (eventually Lord) Pitt, the tireless black political strategist who, in much the same gentle but determined fashion (though with greater use of party politics) used his respected position and mild mannered approach to call for and bring about change on racial matters in the 1970s and 1980s.

Inevitably, given his unusual and outstanding position as a black man in British society – and as an exponent of self-government in the West Indies – much attention has focused on Constantine's contribution to racial politics. But his greatness encompassed more than just his activism, his list of 'firsts' or his cricketing prowess. He was, by common consensus, actually a great man. His friend Dingle Foot wrote after his death, in *The Times*, that he had 'never met anyone who inspired more widespread affection among all sorts and conditions of people'. Sir Roy Wilson, acting chairman of the Race Relations Board at the time of Constantine's death, said he was 'a truly great and truly loveable man', while Noel Wild remembered him as 'the epitome of sunshine and laughter'. The extent and depth of Constantine's popularity was simply extraordinary. His appeal spread across the board; he was equally loved by the man on the street as by the judge in his chambers.

A number of words habitually attach themselves to any descriptions of Constantine – warmth, charm, integrity, good humour, sincerity, consideration, kindness, honour, humanity, enthusiasm. But the list of more negative words is thin indeed. He was sometimes opinionated, but then was also often very accommodating of other people's views. Occasionally he could be over-protective of his reputation; then again he was nearly always modest about his achievements, especially those outside cricket. Sometimes he was perhaps too trusting.

Constantine, as CLR James observed, was not just 'one of the most remarkable personalities of the day' but 'a man of character'. He was a devoted husband and father, a loyal and generous friend,

Radical stance: although superficially an establishment figure, Constantine was, in cricket as in life, reluctant to accept the status quo

a good storyteller, always fine company, a man who, according to *Wisden*, 'maintained his high moral standards unswervingly'. Although he was always in demand for a handshake and a chat from members of the public, he was courteous to his admirers, never aloof, never given to airs and graces. He could hardly have received more honours, yet was always down to earth. Sam Morris maintained that 'no amount of recognition and honour made any dent in Learie's armour of humility and modesty'. He was especially loved by children, just as much in England, where he delighted the kids of Nelson with joy rides in his Austin Seven, as in Trinidad, where as a politician on school visits he would entertain classes with magic tricks. Howat, who talked of Constantine's 'essential friendliness' noted that 'there were qualities of honesty and simplicity in him which belonged to the nature of a child, and which never deserted him'.

It is easy for a successful sportsperson to become an object of affection, especially one who has been so entertaining on the field of play. But Constantine's popularity stemmed from his joyful, friendly and engaging personality, not just from his time on the cricket pitch. He spent many subsequent years saying and doing things that could easily have lost him his popularity, but it never waned. If anything, it increased. He was, quite simply, a very likeable and admirable man. 'Much has been said about Learie Constantine the cricketer,' said the *Trinidad & Tobago Express* on his death. 'But it was as a man that he really left his mark. His special attribute was his warmth and human understanding. He was a great man who lived with dignity and courage.'

Constantine's attractive personality did not extinguish or even mask his ambition and passion – it allowed him, as *Wisden* said, to fight discrimination against his people 'with a dignity firm but free from acrimony'. It also helped him become a legendary figure in his own lifetime, not just in one territory but in several. He left the world much admired, much respected, much loved.

Bibliography

100 Great West Indian Test Cricketers, Bridgette Lawrence, Hansib, 1988.

A Cricket Pro's Lot, Fred Root, Edward Arnold & Co, 1937.

A Corner of a Foreign Field: the Indian History of a British Sport, Ramachandra Guha, Picador, 2002.

A History of West Indies Cricket, Michael Manley, Andre Deutsch, 1995.

A Look at Learie Constantine, Undine Giuseppi, Thomas Nelson & Sons, 1974.

A Man for All Cultures: the Careers of Learie Constantine, Angus Calder in: Sport in Society, vol 6, No1 (March 2003), pages 19–42.

A Nation Imagined: First West Indies Test Team, the 1928 Tour, Hilary Beckles, Ian Randle Publishers, 2003.

An Area of Conquest: Popular Democracy and West Indies Cricket Supremacy, Hilary Beckles, (ed) Ian Randle Publishers, 1994.

Beyond a Boundary, CLR James, Yellow Jersey Press, 2005.

Beyond the Mother Country: West Indians and the Notting Hill White Riots, Edward Pilkington, I B Tauris & Co, 1988.

Caribbean Cricketers, Clayton Goodwin, George Harrap & Co, 1980.

Colour Bar, Learie Constantine, Stanley Paul, 1954.

Cricket, CLR James (ed: Anna Grimshaw), Allison & Busby, 1986.

Cricket and I, Learie Constantine, Philip Allan, 1933.

Cricket Crackers, Learie Constantine, Stanley Paul, 1950.

Cricket in the Leagues, John Kay, Eyre & Spottiswoode, 1970.

Cricket in the Sun, Learie Constantine, Stanley Paul, 1948.

Cricketers' Carnival, Learie Constantine, Stanley Paul, 1948.

Cricketers' Cricket, Learie Constantine, Eyre & Spottiswoode, 1949.

Game of a Lifetime, Denzil Batchelor, Northumberland Press, 1953.

Learie Constantine, Gerald Howat, Allen & Unwin, 1975.

Liberation Cricket: West Indies Cricket Culture, H Beckles & B Stoddart (eds), Ian Randle Publishers, 1995.

Lord Constantine & Sir Hugh Wooding, A M Clarke, HEM Publishers, 1982.

Muscular Learning: Cricket and Education in the Making of the British West Indies at the End of the 19th Century, Clem Seecharan, Ian Randle Publishers, 2006.

Nelson Cricket Club 1878–1978, centenary brochure, 1978.

See the Conquering Hero: the Story of the Lancashire League 1892–1991, David Edmundson, Mike McLeod Publishing, 1992.

Staying Power: The History of Black People in Britain, Peter Fryer, Pluto Press, 1984.

The Changing Face of Cricket, Learie Constantine & Denzil Batchelor, Eyre & Spottiswoode, 1966.

The Development of West Indies Cricket, volume one: The Age of Nationalism, Hilary Beckles, University of the West Indies Press, 1998.

The Development of West Indies Cricket, volume two: the Age of Globalization, Hilary Beckles, University of the West Indies Press, 1998.

The Elusive Eric Williams, Ken Boodhoo, Ian Randle Publishers, 2001.

198

The Greatest Show on Turf, Noel Wild, Hendon Publishing, Nelson, 1992.

The Rise of West Indian Cricket: from Colony to Nation, Frank Birbalsingh, Hansib, 1996.

The Young Cricketer's Companion: The Theory and Practice of Joyful Cricket, Learie Constantine, Souvenir Press, 1964.

Windrush: The Irresistible Rise of Multi-racial Britain, Trevor Phillips & Mike Phillips, HarperCollins, 1999.

Statistics
Sir Learie Constantine

A statistical review by Andrew Hignell
(Secretary of the Association of Cricket Statisticians
– with grateful thanks to http://cricketarchive.com/)

Full name: Learie Nicholas Constantine

Born: 21st September 1901, Petit Valley, Diego Martin, Trinidad
Died: 1st July 1971, Brondesbury, Hampstead, London, England

First Class Career Record (1921/22-1945)

Batting and Fielding

M	I	NO	Runs	HS	Ave	100/50	Ct
119	197	11	4475	133	24.05	5/28	133

Bowling

Balls	Mdns	Runs	Wkts	BB	Ave	5wI/10wM
17458	481	8991	439	8-38	20.48	25/4

First Class Record Season-by-Season

Season	M	I	NO	Runs	HS	Ave	100/50	Ct
1921–22 (West Indies)	1	2	0	24	24	12.00	–/–	1
1922–23 (West Indies)	2	4	0	58	17	14.50	–/–	1
1923 (England)	20	31	4	425	77	15.74	–/2	15
1923–24 (West Indies)	2	4	0	38	25	9.50	–/–	–
1924–25 (West Indies)	2	4	0	37	36	9.25	–/–	4
1925–26 (West Indies)	5	8	1	99	29	14.14	–/–	2
1926–27 (West Indies)	1	2	0	24	13	12.00	–/–	2
1927–28 (West Indies)	3	4	0	135	63	33.75	–/1	1
1928 (England)	26	43	3	1381	130	34.52	3/10	33
1928–29 (West Indies)	3	5	0	224	133	44.80	1/1	10
1929–30 (West Indies)	5	10	0	144	52	14.40	–/1	16
1930–31 (Australia)	13	23	0	708	100	30.78	1/5	21
1933 (England)	5	9	0	181	64	20.11	–/2	5
1934–35 (India)	2	3	0	30	17	10.00	–/–	–
1934–35 (West Indies)	5	9	0	296	90	32.88	–/2	5
1938-39 (West Indies)	1	2	0	12	11	6.00	–/–	–
1939 (England)	22	32	3	614	79	21.17	–/4	17
1945 (England)	1	2	0	45	40	22.50	–/–	–

Season	Balls	Mdns	Runs	Wkts	BB	Ave	5wI/10wM
1921–22 (West Indies)	126	4	44	2	2–44	22.00	–/–
1922–23 (West Indies)	318	13	109	4	2–7	27.25	–/–
1923 (England)	1472	39	809	37	5–48	21.86	1/–
1923–24 (West Indies)	290	15	109	12	8–38	9.08	1/1
1924–25 (West Indies)	115	6	48	0	–	–	–/–
1925–26 (West Indies)	540	15	284	12	4–52	23.66	–/–
1926–27 (West Indies)	348	5	211	3	2–55	70.33	–/–
1927–28 (West Indies)	369	10	202	11	5–32	18.36	1/–
1928 (England)	4341	131	2456	107	7–45	22.95	6/2
1928–29 (West Indies)	638	24	309	21	5–64	14.71	1/–
1929–30 (West Indies)	1133	47	572	21	5–87	27.23	1/–
1930–31 (Australia)	1802	25	950	47	6–25	20.21	3/–
1933 (England)	700	26	310	14	5–44	22.14	1/–
1934–35 (India)	?	?	254	15	6–72	16.93	1/–
1934–35 (West Indies)	1024	46	344	25	4–40	13.76	1/–
1938–39 (West Indies)	152	6	69	4	4–41	17.25	–/–
1939 (England)	3964	67	1831	103	7–49	17.77	9/1
1945 (England)	126	2	80	1	1–53	80.00	–/–

First Class Record for Each Team

Batting and Fielding

Team	M	I	NO	Runs	HS	Ave	100/50	Ct
Barbados	1	2	0	12	11	6.00	–/–	–
British Guiana and Trinidad	1	1	0	38	38	38.00	–/–	1
CA Wiles' XII	1	2	0	86	63	43.00	–/1	–
Dominions	1	2	0	45	40	22.50	–/–	–
Freelooters	2	3	0	30	17	10.00	–/–	–
Rest of West Indies	1	1	0	11	11	11.00	–/–	–
Trinidad	17	32	1	604	133	19.48	1/2	24
West Indians	74	116	10	2943	130	27.76	4/21	73
West Indies	20	36	0	673	90	18.69	–/4	29
West Indies XI	1	2	0	33	17	16.50	–/–	6

Bowling

Team	Balls	Mdns	Runs	Wkts	BB	Ave	5wI/10wM
Barbados	152	6	69	4	4–41	17.25	–/–
British Guiana and Trinidad	66	2	18	2	2–18	9.00	–/–
CA Wiles' XII	129	5	58	7	5–32	8.28	1/–
Dominions	126	2	80	1	1–53	80.00	–/–
Freelooters	?	?	254	15	6–72	16.93	1/–
Rest of West Indies	174	3	126	2	1–37	63.00	–/–
Trinidad	2403	87	1065	55	8–38	19.36	2/1
West Indians	10363	241	5304	283	7–45	18.74	19/3
West Indies	3793	129	1875	65	5–75	28.84	2/–
West Indies XI	252	6	142	5	4–66	28.40	–/–

Career Record for the West Indies in Test Cricket (1928–1939)

Batting and Fielding

M	I	NO	Runs	HS	Ave	100/50	Ct
18	33	0	635	90	19.24	0/4	28

Bowling

Balls	Mdns	Runs	Wkts	BB	Ave	5wI/10wM
3583	125	1746	58	5–75	30.10	2/–

Test Batting and Fielding Against Each Opponent

Batting and fielding

Opponent	M	I	NO	Runs	HS	Ave	100/50	Ct
Australia	5	10	0	72	14	7.20	–/–	9
England	13	23	0	563	90	24.47	–/4	19

Bowling

Opponent	Balls	Mdns	Runs	Wkts	BB	Ave	5wI/10wM
Australia	765	15	407	8	2–50	50.87	–/–
England	2818	110	1339	50	5–75	26.78	2/–

Test Matches Played by Learie Constantine

Date	Series	Test	Venue
23rd Jun 1928	West Indies in England	1st Test England v W.Indies	Lord's Cricket Ground, London
21st Jul 1928	West Indies in England	2nd Test England v W.Indies	Old Trafford, Manchester
11th Aug 1928	West Indies in England	3rd Test England v W.Indies	The Oval, London
11th Jan 1930	England in West Indies	1st Test W.Indies v England	Kensington Oval, Barbados
1st Feb 1930	England in West Indies	2nd Test W.Indies v England	Queen's Park Oval, Port of Spain
21st Feb 1930	England in West Indies	3rd Test W.Indies v England	Bourda, Georgetown
12th Dec 1930	West Indies in Australia	1st Test Australia v W.Indies	Adelaide Oval
1st Jan 1931	West Indies in Australia	2nd Test Australia v W.Indies	Sydney Cricket Ground
16th Jan 1931	West Indies in Australia	3rd Test Australia v W.Indies	Exhibition Ground, Brisbane
13th Feb 1931	West Indies in Australia	4th Test Australia v W.Indies	Melbourne Cricket Ground
27th Feb 1931	West Indies in Australia	5th Test Australia v W.Indies	Sydney Cricket Ground
22nd Jul 1933	West Indies in England	2nd Test England v W.Indies	Old Trafford, Manchester
24th Jan 1935	England in West Indies	2nd Test W.Indies v England	Queen's Park Oval, Port of Spain
14th Feb 1935	England in West Indies	3rd Test W.Indies v England	Bourda, Georgetown
14th Mar 1935	England in West Indies	4th Test W.Indies v England	Sabina Park, Kingston
24th Jun 1939	West Indies in England	1st Test England v W.Indies	Lord's Cricket Ground, London
22nd Jul 1939	West Indies in England	2nd Test England v W.Indies	Old Trafford, Manchester
19th Aug 1939	West Indies in England	3rd Test England v W.Indies	The Oval, London

Constantine at Nelson:

Season	runs	average	wickets	average
1929	820	34.16	88	9.12
1930	621	38.00	73	10.40
1931	801	50.00	91	9.00
1932	476	22.66	91	8.15
1933	1000	52.63	96	8.50
1934	657	36.50	90	8.28
1935	493	30.81	79	10.50
1936	632	33.26	86	11.22
1937	863	43.15	82	11.11

Source: G Howat

Index